THE BATTLES OF WALES

Dilys Gater

GWASG CARREG GWALCH

ISBN: 0-86381-178-7

Cover design: Anne Lloyd Morris

First published in 1991 by Gwasg Carreg Gwalch,
Capel Garmon, Llanrwst, Gwynedd, Wales.

Tel: 06902 261

THE BATTLES OF WALES

To my dear and precious family,
my husband Stanley, and the cats Who and Patch,
who saw me safely through the writing of this book.

CONTENTS

AUTHOR'S NOTE

It would have been impossible to write this account of the battles of Wales without reference to the many scholarly and detailed works on this subject by previous authors — a selected list of which appears at the end of this volume.

I should like to express my gratitude to the authors of all the books and articles I consulted, and should also like to thank the following people whose assistance helped so much to make my task easier:

Chris Owen at Aberystwyth, whose efficient research provided the answers to many questions;

Wendy Lynne Hughes, who unearthed copies of articles from her own files and willingly encouraged me to make use of them;

Peggy Poole, who as always, assisted wherever she could;

Myrddin ap Dafydd, my publisher, whose assistance, encouragement and confidence in my abilities brought me through many difficult moments.

INTRODUCTION

The Welsh people are descended from antiquity; from dark, tempestuous Iberian seafarers, who settled here over two thousand years before Christ; from the Bronze Age Beaker Folk who brought their skills in working metal and making pottery, and from tall blond Celts with their fair skin and speedwell-blue eyes, who were driven northwards from Gaul by the Romans. Harried later by other invaders to English shores, the Celts held the mountain fastnesses of Scotland and Wales, and the far distances of Cornwall and Brittany. With their characteristic dreams and temperament of fire and passion, their love of colour, their vision and their language which made them a race apart, the Welsh, from an old Teutonic word meaning "foreigner", called themselves the *Cymry*, "the brotherhood".

From this ancient melting-pot of turbulence and strife, rich with legend and overlaid with mysticism, was born the land we know as Wales and the people we know as Welsh. All through the centuries, successive English monarchs tried to conquer Wales and subdue its people. The Welsh knew what oppression meant — there are more castles per square mile in their country than in any other country in the world. In spite of the iron fist of castles looming through the mist, the records of bloodshed, the Parliamentary acts which pronounced that Wales no longer existed as a separate country, the Welsh refused to be conquered. Cross the border and by-pass the bulk of the great Dyke built in the eighth century by Offa, King of Mercia to mark the furthest reaches of his territory, into which no Welshman could cross on pain of death, and you will know at once that you are in a "foreign" land; even the air is different. Battles and slaughter there have been, and nearly every inch of Welsh soil is drenched in blood where the *Cymry* fought to preserve the freedom of their land and the sovereignty of their princes. But in spite of a certain amount of conformity and compromise, Wales remains free, and somewhere in legend-shrouded caves in the mountains, the torchlight gleams softly on the silent figures of Arthur and his knights as they wait until the day they may be needed to ride out once more and defend their country against the invader; somewhere, the spirit of Owain Glyndŵr, hand on his sword, listens for the summons to take up once again the cause of his people.

In ancient days, the tales of the great battles were sung in the halls of the princes and chieftains after meat, and the bard who composed them

9

was honoured even by the prince himself. So was history chronicled and the exploits of great men and their deeds passed on. Today we are more prosaic, yet if we imagine the firelight flickering and mingling with the sparks from the torches, throwing shadow into the dark corners; the gleam of a jewel, and an indrawn breath as the harp sings and the bard's voice recounts to a silent assembly tales of courage and valour, betrayal and blood and death — this is the rightful setting for any account of the Battles of Wales.

Chapter One

THE BATTLES WITH ROME

There are almost no records of the earliest battles that took place on Welsh soil. Previous to the coming of the Romans the whole of Britain was inhabited by large numbers of tribes who probably had little knowledge of anywhere except their own small tracts of land, though they did have some sort of social system, with the tribes being ruled by "royal" families and an upper class of freemen. Subject to them were the serfs, who were little better than slaves.

Names emerge from the murk of these primitive times like jewels being brought out of a dark cave to glitter in the light. Shakespeare's *Cymbeline* lived in south-eastern Britain in the person of Cunobelinus, who was known as "King of the Britons". One thing which we can be sure of, however, is that none of the tribesmen who then inhabited the land we know today as Wales, the dark Iberians whose ancestors had come from the Mediterranean, the Celts with their flowing flaxen hair and fiercely blue eyes, and the various other nomadic tribesmen who had settled in the wild country to the west of Britain, would have ever admitted that Cunobelinus was any king of theirs. They were too busy surviving and making sure that their animals, horses, cattle, sheep, survived, and skirmishing with their neighbours to bother about such refinements as kings and culture.

At this time, Wales was roughly divided into four parts which were later perpetuated in the four Welsh dioceses of Bangor, St Asaph, St David's and Llandaff. In the south and south-east, the dark-browed descendants of the Iberian nomads formed the tribe called the Silures. Northward from them dwelt the Ordivices, who were known as the "Hammermen" because they swept into battle with the formidable weapons of flint-headed hammers to harry their foes. Westwards lived the Demaete, and in the mountain fastnesses of Snowdonia and on the isle of Anglesey, many smaller tribes clung to their pieces of land. Anglesey, known as Mona, was the sacred isle of the Druids or spiritual leaders of the people, where according to rumour among the Roman invaders, horrible rites such as human sacrifice which stained the altars with blood were carried out, along with magic and soothsaying, since the tribes worshipped their own strange Gods.

Once the Romans set about the subjugation of Britain in real

11

earnest, Wales received the first of its heroes whose battles were to become celebrated. This was none other than Prince Caractacus, one of the sons of King Cunobelinus, who fled westward when his father's kingdom, which had by this time passed to himself and his brother, was seized by the Roman general Aulus Plautius. In the south-east, all was lost, but Caractacus (in Welsh — Caradog) rallied the Silures and the Ordovices to resist efforts to conquer Wales. The Romans were very anxious to do this because of Wales' valuable mines which had been known for years to traders who had dared to sail into the northern mists to trade and barter.

For several years, Caractacus led the Silures and the Ordovices as a sort of guerilla leader, as the Romans tried to break through into Wales, and though no battles as such are recorded during this time we can imagine how many skirmishes there were with Roman troops being fiercely ambushed by the tall, blond Prince with his flowing hair beneath his helmet, urging on the yelling bands of Silures, who possessed no such weapons as the Roman sword and shield, but who made up for this by the fury of their attacks, the element of surprise as they seemed to emerge, apparently from nowhere to harry their foes.

At last, however, the might of Rome proved too strong, and Caractacus was defeated in a bitterly fought out "last stand". Shropshire, where one hill is still named Caer Caradoc, is popularly supposed to have been where this battle took place, but other authorities set the scene on Cefn Carnedd, between Llanidloes and Caersws, or at Dolforwyn Castle near Newtown. All these are possibilities, but the site of Caractacus' defeat has never really been positively identified.

The Prince was not killed in the battle, but managed to escape and flee northward to the Brigantes in Yorkshire, among whom he sought sanctuary, but their Queen, Cartimandua, (a sort of British Jezebel by all accounts), betrayed him and handed him over to the Romans. He was taken to Rome and paraded in chains, but the dignity with which he met this humiliating fate saved his life, and because of his great nobility of bearing as he was mocked at by the gleeful Roman populace, the Emperor granted him a free pardon for the awful crime of trying to defend his homeland against invaders.

Meanwhile, though their leader had been forced to leave them to fight on alone, the tribesmen of Wales continued to remain undefeated in spite of all the efforts of the Roman general Ostorius Scapula to subdue them. By 49 A.D., most of Southern England was under

Roman rule, and the legions had reached northwards as far as the Trent, and in the west to the Dee and the Severn, and Ostorius (whose defeat of Caractacus had been hailed in Rome as among the greatest victories any Roman general had ever achieved) tried to consolidate his position by building a camp at Caerleon-on-Usk. He found this task almost impossible, since his troops were mercilessly harried by the Welsh tribesmen, who would appear so unexpectedly from their rocky and wooded fastnesses, and even though badly-armed, and dressed only in skins and furs, would ambush and scatter working parties, terrorise the Roman auxiliaries and generally create havoc among the disciplined troops who found themselves unable to deal with such guerilla tactics. Just as questions were being asked in Rome about why a few natives were able to defy the might of the legions, and plans were being mooted to hunt down and exterminate the whole troublesome lot of them, Ostorius fell ill and died. His death had not occurred in battle, but round the camp-fires of the Welsh, the Silures and the Ordovices, glittering-eyed with triumph, told each other that it was their victory just the same, since it was obviously worry about the war that had killed him. It may well have been, and for several years after his death, no further action was taken to try and conquer Wales, though the Roman camps at Chester and Wroxeter kept the ambushes and aggressive activities of the tribesmen under a certain amount of control. Guerilla activities on the part of the Welsh continued to be a thorn in the side of what Rome now regarded as another of its "provinces", and a peaceful settlement of Britain.

Though an account of these early battles is impossible to give since there are few or no records of the clashes, the Roman historian Tacitus did describe in vivid words what happened when, about eight years after the death of Ostorius, another general, Suetonius Paulinus, led the legions westwards from Chester in an effort to capture Anglesey. As well as being the sacred isle of the Druids, Anglesey was noted for the fact that it was where fugitives from justice sought shelter, and so was probably considered a hot-bed of unrest.

It was never the policy of the tribesmen to stand against detachments of armed forces in a pitched battle if they could help it, and as Suetonius and his men pressed further and further into North Wales, sunlight glinting from spear and sword, the well-trained feet of the legionaries marching in step through the wild countryside, the eagle of Rome at their head, the tribesmen melted quietly into the woods and withdrew into the mountains inland. Many times the high peaks of

13

Snowdonia — the Welsh *Eryri* — were to provide a stronghold that could not be conquered or captured from which Welsh armies could sally forth against their enemies, but the tribesmen knew better than to try and throw themselves against Roman might this time. They remained in hiding and Suetonius at length led his troops as far as the Menai Straits, where flat-bottomed boats were made ready to transport the foot-soldiers to Anglesey shore. The cavalry urged their horses into the water and remained astride their mounts as the beasts swam across the Straits. Tacitus describes what followed:

> "On the shore stood the forces of the enemy, a dense array of arms and men, with women dashing through the ranks like the furies; their dress was funeral, their hair dishevelled, and they carried torches in their hands. The Druids around the host, pouring forth dire imprecations with their hands uplifted towards the heavens, struck terror into the soldiers by the strangeness of the sight; insomuch that, as if their limbs were paralysed, they exposed their bodies to the weapons of the enemy without attempting to move."

The Romans were just as superstitious in their own way as any of the wild tribes they conquered, and possibly Tacitus thought that an account of a Roman victory would sound all the better if he could persuade his readers that the enemy was backed up by powerful and mystic priests of a horrific alien religion. Armed men certainly would never have stopped the legionaires in their tracks with horror, but the unusual sight of women among the warriors, hair streaming in the wind and the lights of their torches, and the awesome figures of the Druids calling down their Gods to protect them and cursing their enemies, would have given the readers as well as the troops who were attacking Anglesey the distinct impression that the forces of Suetonius had been faced by a terrible and practically supernatural horde on Anglesey's shore. However, in spite of their shock at the reception they were getting, the legionaires did not hesitate for long. Tacitus continues:

> "At the earnest exhortations of the general, and from the effect of their own mutual importunities that they would not be scared by a rabble of women and fanatics, they bore down upon them, smote all who opposed them to the earth, and wrapped them in the flames they had themselves kindled."

In other words, the Romans upon landing, slaughtered everyone who tried to stand in their way, including the women and the unarmed

Druids. Blood would have stained the Straits fiercely crimson that day, and a pall of dark smoke from the fires on which the dead and dying bodies were unceremoniously thrown hung over the shameful scene.

Even as the last helpless figures slumped on the sands twitched and moaned in their dying agonies, and the high-piled funeral pyres burned themselves out, Suetonius' men over-ran the island, dragging forth cowering victims who tried to hide, tearing down the sacred oak-groves, and smashing the altars where the Druids had carried out their rites. Tacitus sums this up in one line:

> "A garrison was then established to over-awe the vanquished, and the groves dedicated to their bloody superstitions destroyed."

But as Anglesey shuddered beneath the heel of Rome, despoiled, ravaged and lost, Suetonius received news that caused him to withdraw hastily with his troops. Under their Queen, Boadicea, the Iceni and other tribes in the south-east of Britain had rebelled and the province was in revolt. While Boadicea (in Welsh — Buddug) and her followers engaged the legions in their chariots with knives on the wheels, their faces and bodies painted with blue woad, shrieking defiance, Wales nursed its wounds. And for another ten years, while the whole province recovered from the aftermath of terrible bloodshed in which seventy thousand of the troops had been cut down by the furious southerly tribes, and Suetonius had retaliated by slaughtering more than that number of Britons, the province was quiet. On the surface, at least. Though further troubles were in store, and in the end, the Romans were to consider they had conquered the wild land to the west, which had held out against them for so long.

The valuable Welsh mines were what tempted Rome to make renewed efforts against the Silures and the Ordovices, and between 74 A.D. and 78 A.D., the "conquest" of Wales was accomplished by two generals, Julius Frontinus and his successor Julius Agricola, who happened to be the father-in-law of the historian Tacticus, Frontinus determined to subdue the troublesome Silures of South Wales, possibly to prove that he was as good a general as his predecessor Petilius Cerealis, who had scored great victories over the Brigantes in Yorkshire and brought them to heel. Frontinus set out to do the same with the Silures, in spite of their undoubted bravery and the fact that their country was difficult for campaigns. By means which have not been recorded, he managed to completely subdue South Wales, though the northern tribes remained just as much of a worry as ever. It was left to Agricola, who arrived on the scene in 78 A.D., to tackle the notorius Hammermen and the hordes who occupied the mountain fastnesses of Snowdonia, as well as the new population that had established itself in Anglesey since Suetonius' troops had slaughtered the Druids and their supporters and torn down the sacred groves.

Just before Agricola arrived, the Ordovices had successfully attacked a squadron of cavalry stationed somewhere within their territory, and almost wiped it out, with only a few survivors who were able to tell the tale. Agricola, notwithstanding the fact that the soldiers were anticipating withdrawal to their winter quarters and the troops were scattered over the province, organised a force of picked men and led them himself into the mountains of Snowdonia. The tribesmen, bearded, as it were, in their lair, into which no enemy had ever dared to venture before, fell before his advance, fighting to the death, but unable to stop the invaders from successfully capturing their strongholds. Having practically wiped out the fighting force of the tribe, Agricola's victorious army marched on to the coast, where, since there was no fleet to back up his attack on Anglesey, he used the same tactics that had proved effective for Suetonius, and launched a surprise attack with auxiliary troops astride their horses swimming across the Straits.

Utterly disheartened, Anglesey surrendered, and the "conquest" of Wales was complete. Agricola pressed on the next year to consolidate his northern forts and garrisons and later to proceed into Scotland where he inflicted crushing defeats on the tribes there.

During the three centuries that Wales, as well as most of the rest of Britain, remained under Roman rule, two of the three legions which were stationed in the province were posted on the Welsh border, presumably because it was thought that Wales might prove more troublesome than anywhere else without a sharp eye being kept on what was going on there. But there were no more battles in Wales during this time. The precious mines came under Roman control, and the enslaved Welsh tribesmen toiled unceasingly, though no doubt resentfully, under their Roman masters to produce the ore, which was sent off to swell the Emperor's coffers. Forts and garrisons were built, and a network of roads linked them, but no effort was made to colonise the wild country, and so long as they behaved themselves, the tribes who lived in the hills were left alone to carry on in the old ways. National pride began to dawn, and bards wandered from camp to camp with golden words on their lips of ancestral Gods, Goddesses, prophets and enchantresses, stories from the mists of time that linked the people together in a common heritage. This state of affairs would not last for ever, the bards promised, some time their great leader would rise and carry them and Wales with him to glory. A conquered people they might be, but the dreams that shook the hearts of those who sat round fires and listened as the bards sang would never be conquered. In the deepest recesses of the woods and the mountains, the spirit of Wales lived on, unshackled and free.

The Eagles Depart

I, Paulinus am old, at fifty I'm old,
And when I peer to the future it is not to this word I look;
My days here below almost over,
Enough for me to obey and to bide my hour.
And when I look back I behold how vainly I've striven.
Heavy my days have been,
Memories of youth remain my only delight.
Four years old was I in my father's arms in Caerleon
Gazing at the host of Maxen and Helen the Arvonian Empress
Marching out of my city,
Under the eyes of the city,
Over the ringing stones of Sarn Helen out of the sound of the city.
Said my father, behold the world we have known is no more,
The long-established motion of the sun is no more,
Stability we shall know no more,
No more the carving of stones for the long-lasting dwellings,
The endless ages of Rome and her peace are no more.
And my father wept.
But my mother replied:
When Rome's tranquillity is gone, the Peace of our Lord shall stand.
The daily oblations of Christian priests are the stones of our city's construction,
And our civilisation shall stand united and paved by the unshaken Creed.
Truly she spoke. For then,
Bereft of centurions and legions and the eagle banners,
And left in our weakness to hold the border,
The barbarians venturing nearer and ever nearer across the land,
And the Scots ever bolder and bolder from over the sea,
Yet in that hour it was that learning and piety
Blossomed like late spring in our land;
To our midst in Dyved and Gwent and Glamorgan
Came a constant stream of sages, teachers of letters and law
From the ravaged lands to the east and the burnt-out cities.

Our lime-washed churches and schools bloom like the cherry-tree's blossom,
And Ambrosius, lord of Caerleon and the South, eagerly welcomes
The heirs of Quintilian and Virgil, the fathers of language,
And the dejected pious disciples of Jerome of Bethlehem.

Saunders Lewis

Chapter Two

THE SLAUGHTER OF THE SAINTS

Early morning with mist hanging low over the still trees, shrouding their vividness. The hills of Wales crouched against the skyline providing a backcloth for the scene unfolding before us as, with all the ritual attendant on this day when many of the actors in the drama will not live to see the hazy sun set behind those hills in the west tonight, two armies prepare for battle. On the air we can hear the jingle of harness, the shrill neigh of a horse, the clash of metal as the warriors arm themselves.

Surrounded by the attentive figures of his captains, the commanding form of Aethelfrith, King of Northumbria, scans the field with narrowed eyes as he measures the might of the opposing forces of the Welsh. Beneath banners which hang limply in the unstirring air, the men of Powys gather in support of their king, Selyf ap Cynan Garwyn; those of eastern Gwynedd are led by Cadwal Crisban of Rhos; in other parts of the field rise the standards of lesser princes.

And, escorted by the grey-bearded yet still flashing-eyed Prince Brochfael Ysgythrog, grandfather of the young Selyf of Powys, a huge crowd of robed and tonsured monks who have walked from the nearby monastery at Bangor-on-Dee take up their positions to lend their countrymen the support of their prayers for a Welsh victory. The sound of their deep-toned chanting fills the air, and Aethelfrith's face contorts with anger as he prepares to lead his forces into battle.

"The monks fight against me as surely as if they bore arms," he declares furiously, and gives the signal to attack. "Spare no-one who stands against us in the field."

Helpless as the troops of Northumbria advance upon them while Brochfael and his followers ride to the support of the main body of the Welsh armies, the monks are swept down like grass beneath a scythe, their prayers still on their lips, empty hands uplifted in entreaty to heaven.

Twelve hundred were cut down in cold blood in this 'slaughter of the saints', only fifty monks managing to escape before the battle between the two armies of Northumbria and Wales was joined in earnest and the horses staggered fetlock-deep in churned-up earth and blood, while the flower of Welsh chivalry fell. By evening, when Aethelfrith triumphantly surveyed the field, Selyf and Cadwal lay dead, their sightless eyes and those of the men who had fallen with them seeming to try vainly to pierce the dusk for a last glimpse of the hills of the country they had given their lives to defend from the invader. Selyf was the first Welsh king to lay down his life against the English in defence of his homeland. And as word spread along the valleys of the Dee and the Severn, the bards mourned to hushed listeners of this darkest of dark days for Wales and her princes, tales of the battle that would keep the memory of those fallen heroes green for as long as their songs were remembered, and celebrate the cruel slaughter of twelve hundred men of God who had been murdered as they prayed for their countrymen.

After the Roman legions were withdrawn from Britain at the beginning of the fifth century, the native Britons were left to defend themselves as best they could against ferocious attacks from all sides, including raids southward by the wild Pictish tribes in Scotland, who had never really been properly subjugated. Over the two centuries that followed, England was invaded repeatedly by Saxons who harried the eastern coasts, eventually sweeping in a great tide to settle all over the country, driving the Britons westwards, as the Romans had previously driven the Celts, into Wales, Cornwall and the western parts of Northern England.

As if this was not enough, Wales was also invaded from the west by tribes from Ireland who were called Goidels or Gaels, and who were blood-thirsty and barbaric. There had already been a certain amount of settlement by Irish tribes who had established themselves particularly in Dyfed, with the result that many of the Welsh kings and princes were claimed to be descended from Irish chiefs, but, not satisfied with small settlements, the Goidels over-ran the whole of North Wales and in spite of Welsh efforts to drive them back, seemed all set to seize the whole of Wales.

In order to prevent this, a Brythonic general called Cunedda came to the rescue with his eight sons and with armies at his back, sweeping down from the north and ruthlessly driving out the Goidels. Cunedda then established himself as ruler and protector of all the territory between the Dee and the Teifi, and set up his court at Deganwy. He divided his lands between his sons, and the names of the districts were taken from the names of their new princes. Ceredigion (*Cardiganshire*) was the land given to Cunedda's son Ceredig; another son Edeyrn ruled the Vale of Edeyrnion near Corwen; and Cunedda's grandson

Meirion is remembered in the name of Meirionnydd (*Merionethshire*). In effect, this was the founding of the dynasties that would provide Wales with her royal princes and kings for many centuries, and Cunedda's descendants continued to protect their territories, whether against the Goidels or other foes, and to establish their own positions and keep order, administer justice and encourage learning and culture. Wales moved into a Golden Age of heroic chivalry and valour, the bards began to compose some of their loveliest poetry which survives to this day, and even though many of the tribes who were still jostling for supremacy in England were still pagan and had not been converted to Christianity, the church in Wales bloomed, and there were so many holy men that the fifth and sixth centuries are often referred to as 'The Age of Saints'.

We can let our imaginations run wild on the subject of battles during this period, since much of what was fact has been coloured and romanticised by legend and myth, and heroes seem to have been everywhere, leading their men into the fray in gilded armour, with their horses dazzlingly attired in jewelled trappings and banners streaming gold and azure and silver against the sky. Probably the warriors who actually did the fighting were nothing like this romantic picture, and the battles were bloody and hard-fought, with no trace of the chivalric glamour with which the old tales describe them. But heroes who fought for Wales, there certainly were. First Prince Cunedda and his sons, who cleared out the barbaric Goidels, according to the historian Nennius, "with immense slaughter".

Cunedda's grandson Cadwallon Lawhir (*Cadwallon the Longhanded*), continued the war against the Irish invaders, and in about the year 470, he fought the last battle against them in Anglesey. They were never to try to take Wales by force again. It seems to have taken place near Trefdraeth, and according to tradition, Cadwallon and his men were so determined to achieve victory or else die in the attempt that they bound their legs with horses' fetterlocks so that they would not be able to turn and run. A bit less romantic than the gilded armour and the knightly assumption that no true hero ever had any idea of what it was like to feel fear, but this practical tactic worked, and their victory stamped out Irish aggresion completely. The leader of these fearsome barbarians was called Seregri, and during the battle, he was slain. Near to the Parish Church at Holyhead, where there are also the remains of a Roman fort from the Roman occupation of the island, stands a smaller church known as Eglwys y Bedd (*The Church of the*

Grave). Here, so it is said, the bones of the Irish leader lie buried. Presumably Cadwallon honoured his enemy by giving him a burial suitable to his rank, in the best heroic tradition.

One of the kings who actually was ruling in Wales at the time when the knights of legend were weaving their non-existent way to tournaments and to mysterious castles in which beautiful enchantresses sought to imprison them with spells, was Cadwallon Lawhir's son Maelgwn Gwynedd, otherwise known as Maelgwn Hir (*Maelgwn the Tall*), King of Gwynedd and Anglesey. Because of his father's victory over the Irish in Anglesey. Maelgwn was also called 'The Island Dragon', since the power of his family had been conclusively proved on the island, but he was not at all the sort of ruler to fit the heroic picture, though during his lifetime he unified Wales and strengthened her sense of identity as a nation. He also kept a firm grip on law and order, and made sure the lesser kingdoms and princedoms recognised his overlordship, but the means by which he achieved these praiseworthy ends were awful in the extreme, if we can believe Gildas, a monk who wrote a history of Britain.

No actual battles seem to stand out where Maelgwn won victories, he went about his way to supreme authority by far more direct means, namely by murdering such innocent people as stood in his way. It is said that he murdered his wife, the sister of Prince Brochfael Ysgythrog of Powys, and also his nephew, so that he could marry his nephew's wife, and other authorities claim he murdered his uncle so that he could take the crown in the first place, though it seems more likely that he inherited Gwynedd and Anglesey from his father. He was loudly condemned in Gildas' history as the worst of all the bad kings who were ruling in the west at that time (apparently Gildas couldn't find any good ones) and he died in 547 from a terrible Yellow Plague which was then ravaging the countries of Europe — this was held, by Gildas no doubt, if not by others, as a just retribution for his crimes.

Though the rulers of the various Welsh kingdoms and princedoms were now more or less united so that they were not for ever fighting each other, there were quite a lot of arguments (though they didn't end in battles) between the princes and the leaders of the Christian Church in Wales. In fact, a continuous struggle went on between the church and the civil rulers to gain absolute authority over the people. Holy men the saints may have been, but they seem to have been just as anxious as any prince to be regarded as the supreme heads of state who advised on all matters, whether about religion or not.

The church was also divided in Britain because the saints who represented the Roman Church, like Saint Augustine, wanted the British and Welsh Bishops to change their traditional date of Easter, and change other rituals which they had previously observed, as well as do what Augustine said in his position as Archbishop of Canterbury, which involved giving him all the assistance he needed to convert the various heathen kings who had still not stepped into line in England. One cannot blame the Welsh bishops for hesitating, especially as they asked one of their holy men whether they would be right to give up their own traditions and meekly do what Augustine told them, and the answer was that if Augustine really was the meek and lowly man he claimed to be, he would rise from his chair as they approached and not remain seated. But as the delegation of Welsh bishops entered the saint's presence, Augustine showed no inclination to rise and greet them, which persuaded them conclusively that he suffered from the sin of pride, so they decided to keep to their own traditions and told him they did not want him as their archbishop.

Augustine, in a distinctly un-saintly manner, was so annoyed by this that he pronounced a prophetic threat against them. If they would not agree with their brethren peacefully, he said (meaning, if they would not stop arguing with him and refusing to do what he told them) then they would have to suffer war with their enemies. And if they would not help him to show the English the right way to conduct their lives (by which he meant his way), they would lose their own lives as a punishment at the hands of their foes.

It seemed to the historian Bede, when he recorded these events, that the invasion of Wales by the Northumbrian King Aethelfrith and the slaughter of the twelve hundred monks as they knelt in prayer for their countrymen, was a direct fulfilment of the saint's prophecy. This it may or may not have been, but it was the first time any English king actually marched on Wales and attacked it with the intention of bringing it beneath English rule. The year was 616 when the Northumbrian armies loomed ominously on the Welsh horizon, and the battle where the monks were slain and the princes fell in defence of their country took place somewhere near Chester, as the Welsh hurriedly assembled to try and stop Aethelfrith's advance into their territory. We can regard this battle as significant because from this time on, Wales as a nation was to have to defend itself almost continuously against attacks by various kings of England. The wars between the English and the Welsh had begun.

Because there were Welsh kingdoms further north, some in Scotland, as well as those actually in Wales itself, the Battle of Chester is sometimes thought to mark the cutting off for the final time of the Welsh in Wales from their allies and kinsmen the 'Men of the Old North'. In fact, this did not happen directly as a result of Aethelfrith's invasion, as the Northumbrian king died the following year, and was not able to build on his victory by conquering even more of Wales. It was left to his successor, Edwin, to renew the attack against Wales, as well as against the northern Welsh kingdoms, but although not only the Welsh in Wales but the northern Welsh of Ystrad Clud (*Strathclyde*), Gododdin which stretched south from the River Forth, and Rheged, the area round the Solway Firth, all fought valiantly to preserve their traditions and their lands, it was in the end only the Welsh in Wales who were able to keep their nation intact against invaders, whether the invasions were bloody battles or more peaceful tactics such as inter-marrying. The Battle of Chester, however, marked the commencement of a centuries-long and bitterly drawn-out struggle by the Welsh to keep their land, their language and their traditions, alive and free from outside domination.

The Alleluia Victory

In the early fifth century, a celebrated battle took place — traditionally either in the area round Carrog, just off the Corwen to Llangollen road in North Wales, or else at Garmon's Field, outside Mold. General vagueness over the actual site of the battlefield can be explained by the fact that this was such a successful battle that all areas would have liked to appropriate it as part of their own particular local history.

The formidable victor here was not a dashing prince, but one of the saints who had come to Wales to oversee the spreading of the gospel. He was Saint Garmon, or, as he is otherwise known, Germanus, Bishop of Auxerre, who not only went about his religious duties with great zeal, but also interfered in politics, to the extent that, when an army of heathen Picts and Saxons advanced into North Wales, it was Germanus who rallied a force of Christian Welshmen to try and stop their advance.

As the opposing armies met, Germanus' troops advanced shouting 'Alleluia' as their war-cry, and this terrified the Picts and Saxons (so we are told) to such an extent that they all turned and ran without striking a blow. Ignominiously, they were scattered to drown in the nearby river, or to be cut down by the triumphant Welsh swords, giving the saint's forces what must have seemed a miraculous victory.

A monument in Mold commemorates the battle, though the date (which is given as 420) is probably inaccurate, as Germanus did not visit the area until several years later. However the tales that lingered over the years in the locality have turned the Alleluia Victory into a dramatic and colourful folk-legend as well as a more prosaic historical fact.

ANEIRIN

Some of the very earliest surviving Welsh poetry celebrating the heroes and their exploits, was written in the Kingdoms of the 'Old North' before those Welsh-speaking kingdoms in Scotland were lost for ever.

The Welsh bard Aneirin lived in the kingdom of Gododdin in Scotland, and served at the court of Mynyddog Mwynfawr, in his capital city Caeredin (Edinburgh). Surviving from about 600 is Aneirin's rich and vivid elegy known as the Gododdin, *which he composed to honour the men of Gododdin who were killed in battle with the Angles at Catterick.*

Gododdin

The men who went to Catterick were thirsty for war
the best mead in their honour might have as well been poison
three hundred ordered out against an army
after all the celebration, silence
and for all the churcing of the priests
death their last reward.

men went to Catterick at dawn
their own fine fettle was the death of them
yellow the mead poured, sweet and treacherous
year long the minstrelsy, the harp strings never stilled
let the blood now that rusts their swords
never be scoured

men went to Catterick, they were famous
their wages they drank from gold cups
a twelve month of festivity
three hundred and sixty three warriors with neck bands of gold
and of these who so jovially joined battle
three came away
the two war-dogs of Aeron
unyielding Cynon
and myself, soaked in blood, to recount it.

Aneirin

Chapter Three

THE MYTH OF ARTHUR

The most romantic figure which lives on in the tales from the Celtic era when heroes were supposedly riding round on their white horses, keeping a watchful eye open for tyrants they could overthrow, maidens they could rescue, or the odd dragon or sea-serpent that might be making a nuisance of itself, is that of King Arthur. He appears in the folk-lore not only of Wales, but of other parts of Britain and even of Europe.

He was, according to the legends, a king whose court was the scene for all that was greatest and best in the swirling romance of the dim Celtic past and the idealistic concepts of the heroic era. His knights assembled where the towers of his court rose — at Camelot, at Caerleon-on-Usk, at Tintagel, or wherever the narrator of his exploits chose to set it — and he inspired his people to deeds of heroism and chivalry, to loyalty to their country and their king so that they were prepared to lay down their lives if necessary to defend their prince's honour and the territories to which they were pledged as champions and defenders.

In the fabled threads of magic, love and honour which the story-tellers of Celtic days wove round this larger-than-life king, Arthur met his end fighting his own people, who were led by the treacherous Medrod, or Mordred, and who was his own kinsman. But though he is supposed to have fallen in battle, no mortal man ever knew the site of Arthur's grave, and in folk-memory, he and his knights live on in some sort of mystic tranced sleep, ghostly protectors of the good and the righteous, of chivalry and honour — and in Welsh tales, of Wales — who will rise again if ever they are needed.

But the facts are quite different. For one thing, nobody knows with any certainty who the real Arthur was — but what does seem certain is that he was not a king. He was not even a prince, and there are no references to him in any of the contemporary documents of the Celtic era when he was supposed to have lived. The only thing we can say for certain is that, according to later sources detailing the events of the sixth century, Arthur — whoever he was — fought in at least two battles, the Battle of Badon (or Mount Badon) and the Battle of Camlan 'in which Arthur and Medrawd (or Modred) fell'.

It appears that the historical Arthur, while not a king or a prince, was one of the great 'warlords' and leaders of horsemen who led the native Celts, or *Brython*, against the invading Saxons in the sixth century. These 'warlords' or guerilla mercenary leaders, were largely of aristocratic birth, and generally landowners. Arthur was probably of Romano-British descent, leading other young men like himself — and bear in mind that only the nobility were able to possess horses to ride, far less to become familiar enough with the animals to be expert riders, so the fact that this was a company of professional horsemen does mark them out as young aristocrats, more than likely wealthy and of noble blood. The living memory of Arthur might have inspired the Brythonic attack on Catterick by a band of noble horsemen drawn together from every corner of the Welsh-speaking world.

These warrior bands called themselves — as I have mentioned briefly earlier — the *Combrogi*, which means 'fellow countrymen' and probably derives from the Latin word for fellow citizens, *cives*. From this came the word the Welsh used to describe themselves, *Cymry*, meaning brothers, and it is significant in that it shows how the Welsh regarded themselves as of Brythonic origin, in contrast to the developing English nation, which was formed of largely Germanic invaders.

But even though we know there was a historical Arthur, and that he fought in the battles of Badon and Camlan — together it appears he fought twelve battles — the information about this great warrior and leader tells us no more. The sites of his battles, even if they have been tentatively identified, are not in Wales. Mount Badon is thought to have been near Bath, though it has also been placed near Wimborne in north Dorset. We have no evidence at all about where Arthur might have lived or had his court, and the only thing we can say for sure is that wherever it was, it was nothing at all as the legends would have us believe, with gilded towers and shining banners as knights rode forth to the jousting, while their ladies gave them favours and looked on.

It has been suggested that the Celtic warlords and their followers regarded their struggle against the Saxon barbarians as a religious crusade — since Arthur and his people were Christians. This would explain why the chroniclers recorded that 'Arthur carried the image of the Holy Mary, the Everlasting Virgin, on his shield' and that he wore 'the Cross of Our Lord Jesus Christ across his shoulders'. It is also possible — maybe even likely — that since he had to find some sort of headquarters, he might have taken up residence in the old Roman stronghold of Caerleon in South Wales. So perhaps there is a shadowy substance to the old tales of Arthur and his ghostly court gathering in Caerleon-on-Usk, where some scenes in the *Mabinogi*, the Welsh collection of heroic legends, are set. Perhaps too there is some hint in historical evidence, sketchy though it is, that the old tales of the search for the Holy Grail and the ideals which were set at Arthur's mythical Camelot might have had some foundation.

But if we have no evidence that Arthur was Welsh, and that none of his battles (with the possible exception of Camlan, which might have been a siege of Caerleon where Arthur was killed defending his base) took place on Welsh soil, why is it that Arthur is one of the great hero-figures in Welsh history? Why is it that legend has placed him and his knights in the deep recesses of Snowdonia to sleep in their mystic trances until they will rise to defend Wales if she is ever in need of their protection?

The invasion of the Saxons was steady and relentless across the south and east of England. But because of the inspiration and the leadership of Arthur and his band of warriors who fought to keep Wales free, it was to be centuries before this Brythonic nation in the west relinquished its independence — to whatever degree — to the overlordship of England. As a result, Welsh folk-lore has perpetuated the legend that Arthur was one of the greatest warriors ever to take up arms and fight for Wales, in defence of the country and the ideals and traditions of its people against an alien culture.

Because Arthur and his people were Christian, and because they were of Romano-British descent, consequently regarding the Saxon invaders as barbarians and heathens, and because they fought for their beliefs and convictions, defending the principles of society as they knew it, they have been immortalised in heroic legends as knightly protectors of all that was fine, noble and cultured. Arthur himself is the symbol of all that is best and noblest in the ideal Christian king.

The bards and poets of ancient Wales began to establish Arthur's position in literature, though it was not until much later that the story of King Arthur and his faithless Queen Guinevere, of Sir Lancelot and Sir Galahad and the Round Table and the quest for the Grail, began to take the form we know today.

In fact, the early stories of Arthur did not deal with his betrayal in love. In Welsh legend, Arthur was a princely figure who roamed the countryside hunting the great boar called the Twrch Trwyth with his dog. Near Builth Wells was a cairn of stones bearing the paw-print of

Arthur's hound Cabal (or Cafall) on the topmost stone. This stone, according to tradition, would if removed, return of its own accord, since Arthur himself had built the cairn and placed the stone with his dog's paw-print on the top. From this ancient cairn comes the name of Carn Cafall, to be found today near Rhayader.

The early Celtic Arthur sailed — as recorded in the *Book of Taliesin* — to attack the Faery Fort (Caer Siddi) far beyond the seas, in a ship called Prydwen. A huge host accompanied him — only seven warriors returned. The mythical Arthur had ceased to be a mortal and had assumed supernatural attributes, so that the tales which were told of his deeds often included giants, monsters and other legendary beasts as well as wizards and magic.

Whatever its actual foundation in historical fact, the story of Arthur never died but grew in power and popularity. From about the twelfth century, the tale spread to other parts of Britain and into Europe. The people of Cornwall and Brittany, who were descendants of the same Brythonic race as the Welsh, had their own legends, and often claimed Arthur as their own hero. Thus Arthur's court is represented in the various myths as having been situated at Tintagel, or even in lands beyond the seas.

In later years, the Arthurian legend was taken up by the chroniclers of the French romances, by English storytellers and poets, and by writers, painters and creators all over Europe who wanted a theme, an ideal, something to stir the blood and bring a spark to the eye. Always Arthur portrayed the fine, the noble, the best in a Christian knight and king. And he was in addition the central heroic figure in a tangled and passionate tale of faithless love, of trust betrayed and romantic ideals shattered. But most of all, Arthur will always symbolise the greatest warrior, the man who was destined to lead his people in a holy and blessed crusade against darkness and ignorance, brutality and sin. He is the man who wields his great sword for the right, for tradition and culture, for harmony and beauty and all that is fair and precious in living, for the beliefs and ideals and dreams of a people of vision and aspiration.

This is how Wales will always remember Arthur, the greatest Celtic warrior to lift arms and fight for the Brythonic cause, and to keep Wales free.

The Grave of King Arthur

I called on the sun, in his noonday height,
By the power and spell a wizard gave:
Hast thou not found, with thy searching light,
The island monarch's grave?

"I smile on many a lordly tomb,
Where Death is mock'd by trophies fair;
I pierce the dim aisle's hallow'd gloom;
King Arthur sleeps not there."

I bade the winds their swift course hold,
As they swept in their strength the mountain's bre'st:
Ye have waved the dragon banner's fold,
Where does its chieftain rest?

There came from the winds a murmured note,
"Not ours that mystery of the world;
But the dragon banner yet shall float
On the mountain breeze unfurl'd."

Answer me then, thou ocean deep,
Insatiate gulf of things gone by,
In thy green halls does the hero sleep?
And the wild waves made reply:

"He sleeps not in our sounding cells,
Our coral beds with jewels pearl'd;
Not in our treasure depths it dwells,
That mystery of the world.

"Long must the island monarch roam,
The noble heart and the mighty hand;
But we shall bear him proudly home
To his father's mountain land."

Chapter Four

THE PRINCES' BATTLES

The majority of Welsh battles have been fought not to carve out new empires or even to attack existing kingdoms such as the English ones. Wales in the main has fought defensively. Right from the dawn of her history, she was threatened by invading Roman armies, by wave after wave of marauding tribes who came from all sides, from the western coasts as well as from the eastern borders with the kingdoms of the Mercians and the Saxons.

After the Battle of Chester in 616 efforts were made to regain the territories which had been lost to the Northumbrian King Aethelfrith and soon afterwards to his successor, Edwin, who pillaged indiscriminately right across Britain, and also sent a successful fleet to Anglesey. The King of Gwynedd, Cadwallon, hastily allied himself with Penda, King of Mercia, and the allies defeated Northumbria in 632 near Doncaster.

But Cadwallon was killed three years later fighting in the north of Britain near the Great Wall, and in the years that followed, Wales and its former ally Mercia became bitter enemies. It was the Mercian King Offa who was responsible for building the famous Dyke which bears his name and which ran from just short of Prestatyn in the north, to Chepstow in the south. Offa's Dyke, which can still be followed today by walkers, was some eighty miles long and was intended to mark the Mercian frontier with Wales. Its purpose was to keep the Welsh out of Offa's territory and out of the 'No Man's Land' that lay between the Welsh and the Mercian boundaries. As it was in the process of being completed in 796, Offa, in charge of his forces near Rhuddlan, was killed, leaving the Mercian Cenwulf as his successor.

But the Welsh not only had to fight to keep their land secure against those who would wrest it from them. The Welsh nation itself has had to struggle in order to exist. At any time in its history, the Welsh nation — whether on the verge of beginning to consolidate itself or when it was already established to some degree — could so easily have been reduced to nothing not only from without, but from within.

There were so many small kingdoms and princedoms within Wales itself where the princes were greedy for power. As we have already seen, not all of them were as admirable as they might have been. But

31

from time to time, a figure did emerge from the ranks of the princes, who was royal in the best sense of the word, and who was able to claim the title of 'King'.

In the year 844, one of the most notable of these Welsh 'Kings' began to rule. He was Rhodri Mawr (*Rhodri the Great*) who had through the advantageous marriages of his far-seeing father as well as himself, gained the lands of Gwynedd, Powys and Seisyllwg for his kingdom. Many lesser princes still squabbled amongst themselves within the boundaries of Wales, but the real enemies to Welsh unity lurked outside the borders. They continued to be the same ones they had been for almost a century — the kings of Mercia, and also the terrifying Norsemen who had begun to attack the western coasts of Britain, seeking pillage and plunder.

It was in 789, so the *Anglo-Saxon Chronicle* recorded, that: '. . . in his [Beorhtric, King of Wessex] days came first three ships of Norwegians from Horthaland: and then the reeve rode thither and tried to compel them to go to the royal manor, for he did not know what they were: and then they slew him. These were the first ships of the Danes to come to England.'

This was the first indication of what was to become a constant threat and terror not only to the kingdoms of the south but to the north and to Wales as well. The Vikings (which was what their fearful victims called them, and which meant simply 'pirate') were driven by a desire for quick plunder and easy living. As well as seizing booty and riches, they also tried to invade the lands where they landed and over-run them, settling in hordes and setting up their own 'kings', backed up by huge armies. Though they did not succeed in over-running Wales, the great kingdoms of Mercia and East Anglia were destroyed and other Anglo-Saxon lordships weakened, and it was only the brilliant leadership of King Alfred of Wessex which saved London and his own kingdom from Viking domination.

Throughout these times, there were numerous battles in Wales, which were recorded in a few brief words to the effect, for instance, that Offa 'slaughtered the men of South Wales', or fought 'against the Britons'. We can only imagine them as rather confused affairs, as were the confrontations between the various Welsh princes.

The twin sons of King Rhodri Molwynog of Wales, for instance, who succeeded their father in 755, spent most of their time fighting each other over the possession of Anglesey, while the lesser princes squabbled between themselves or were overrun by the Mercians. But there seem to have been no especially memorable battles on Welsh soil during their period, and though there was a good deal of ravaging, pillaging and general unease about each fresh group of soldiers who might turn up on your doorstep or within sight of your village, or even each ship that might sail into the bay, nothing systematic was done to defend and protect Wales as a whole.

As a result, Offa's successor, Cenwulf, pressed far south into Dyfed, while in the north it is recorded that he harried Snowdon and burned the ancient seat of the royal families of Gwynedd, Deganwy. These were obviously not pitched battles between two armies, but sad and brutal affairs which left the ordinary Welsh people without homes, without possessions, with their families killed or wounded, their wives and daughters raped or injured. The swift, brutal attacks of the Norsemen were especially dreaded and feared.

The rule of Rhodri Mawr brought a certain amount of peace, and what must have seemed like the dawning of a new era for Wales. Rhodri was a diplomat as well as a warrior king. He was the first man who succeeded in giving Wales a political unity, by means not of threats or intimidation but his successful marriage policies which we have already noted. He attempted to unite all the Welsh princes against the Norsemen (whom the Welsh called 'the black pagans') and even sought an alliance with the Kings of Ireland against this common enemy.

In 856, his forces defeated the Norsemen in a great battle on Anglesey and the Norse leader Gorm (or Horm) was killed. It is more than likely that Rhodri's fleet and land forces were well drilled, well organised and commanded by able leaders who knew their jobs. In all respects, Rhodri was not just a military leader or an upstart, but a man of vision and meticulous attention to detail, whose wisdom and common sense would have been a match for the weight of numbers and savagery of his opponents.

But any feelings of peace and security which might have begun to dawn during the early years of Rhodri's reign were shattered when, in 871, the Danes surged southwards from York — which, together with Dumbarton, was in their hands. The two kingdoms of Wales and Wessex, each under its own notable leader, Rhodri the Great and Alfred the Great, rallied to the defensive. But within a few years, Rhodri was a fugitive in Ireland while Alfred was similarly hiding in Athelney, and when Rhodri did return to Wales, it was as the ally of the dreaded Norsemen in an effort to defeat the armies of Mercia, which had taken his own kingdom.

This legendary king of Wales was killed in about 878 at the age of almost ninety. Amazingly, he did not die peacefully in his bed, but on the battlefield fighting the Mercians, who had penetrated into Anglesey. So the years when the Welsh felt they had a king to unite them came to an abrupt end.

Even while he was alive, Rhodri had maintained a policy of dividing his lands into principalities, each with its own lord. On his death, he left his kingdom to his three sons, who were traditionally the first Welsh princes to wear diadems round their crowns rather than just gold bands. Far from uniting against a common foe, Rhodri's sons soon began to take arms against each other, and in 892, Anarawd, the eldest, marched on his brother Cadell, having joined forces with none other than the English. It is recorded that they laid waste 'the country of Cardigan and the vale of Towy'.

Rhodri's second son was no more honourable than the eldest, and it was he who, on the death of the youngest brother in 901, moved in forcibly to take possession of Powys. The royal kingdom of Rhodri Mawr was all but reduced to nothing, though Rhodri's grandson Hywel Dda (*Hywel the Good*) did succeed in uniting them for a time.

Hywel was the only Welsh ruler to win the title of 'the Good'. He was praised in the chronicles as 'head and glory of all the Britons', and whereas Rhodri had been thanked for his victories over the Vikings by the Frankish King Charles the Great, Hywel went one better. He not only corresponded with notable foreign leaders, but he made a pilgrimage to Rome. It says a great deal for the stability of his kingdom that when he arrived back, it was still there and still intact.

Hywel's main contribution to Welsh unity and pride lies in the fact that he codified the laws of Wales. In spite of all his good intentions, however, it proved very difficult to enforce these laws, and after his death, the country was in a worse state than ever.

The Norsemen continued to attack and pillage along the coasts in the west, and palls of smoke rising from burning churches and villages were a common sight. In the east, English armies marched deep into Gwent, Brycheiniog and Morgannwg, devastating crops and villages. The princes gathered their own small groups of warriors, supporters and dependents around them, and made no effort to join forces. It was too difficult to scrape their own survival, let alone enter into complicated negotiations with other rulers, draw up terms and squabble over treaties and agreements. The enemy might attack at any moment, and the only things they could depend on were their own swords and the swords of the men at their backs.

It must have seemed as though the Dark Ages had descended once again on Wales. There appeared to be no hope of a future except struggle, bitter fighting and eventual domination and defeat by the Norsemen or the English, or both, while the Welsh princes tore each other and their land to pieces. But a new leader eventually arose in this time of great need. His father was Llywelyn ap Seisyllt, who claimed to be descended from the royal line of Rhodri the Great. His mother was the lone woman descendant of that line. Their son was to be one of great heroes of Welsh history — Gruffudd ap Llywelyn.

In 1022, when his father died, Gruffudd inherited a kingdom full of turmoil and unrest. Both the Mercians and the Norsemen continued to plunder and devastate lands where the lesser princes were in revolt against the rightful heir. The early eleventh century was a time of almost never-ending battle, of continual clashing of arms, attacks by foreign invaders, smoke and flames, screams, blood and death.

Gruffudd spent the early years after his father's death in exile in Ireland, and it was not until 1038 that he returned with the resources to challenge the Mercian and Norse invaders and the usurpers who had stolen his inheritance.

Over the next few years, he led his troops into battle to wrest back his kingdom, and won memorable victories — at Rhyd-y-groes in 1039; at Pencader in 1041 and at the mouth of the Tywi near Caerfyrddin in 1044. At Rhyd-y-groes, he drove back the Mercian armies, and his other two great victories were against a rival claimant who had taken his lands. The battle at Pencader won back for Gruffudd the territories of Ceredigion, while his victory near Newport was against the hired mercenaries of his rival, Hywel ab Edwin. By defeating them, he was able to extend his lands to the coast.

Wales had been for centuries the traditional enemy of Mercia, except at such times as a prince decided it would be expedient to ally himself with the Mercian kings. The ever-increasing power of Wessex, in the south-east of England, made Wessex an even more dangerous threat, and Gruffudd foresaw trouble when in 1055, the Earl of Wessex banished the rightful heir to the Mercian earldom, Aelfgar, and gave Mercia to his own brother. Aelfgar promptly fled to Wales to seek Gruffudd's assistance in recovering his inheritance.

Although Mercia was the traditional enemy of Wales, it was obvious to Gruffudd that the combination of the forces of Harold the powerful Earl of Wessex, of a Mercia which was now in the hands of Harold's brother, and of the other enemies who were waiting to seize their own portions of Wales, were growing too strong. Never would he be able to rest easily and nor would any future ruler of Wales, knowing of the strength massed against the Welsh on the other side of the border.

Consequently, Gruffudd made a treaty with Aelfgar, and to seal it, married Aelfgar's daughter Eadgyth. Then he took the initiative and together the allies marched on Hereford, disregarding the forces of the English, which consisted of a mixed army of Norman-English under the Bishop of Hereford, who was himself a Norman. As with the saints, who often led armies into battle, bishops were not necessarily peace-loving, and Bishop Leofgar was playing a very active part when Gruffudd encountered his army just after crossing Offa's Dyke.

The Welsh soon disposed of this feeble assembly, and the bishop was killed. Hereford was sacked and burned. Gruffudd ap Llywelyn had united the whole of Wales as his kingdom — the only Welsh ruler to do this. He was also one of the few Welsh warriors who defeated the English time after time again.

However, Earl Harold of Wessex was in no hurry to attack Wales. When he did take action, in 1062, he had left nothing to chance. He fully intended to put paid to Gruffudd ap Llywelyn for good, and had prepared his whole plan of campaign meticulously.

His army had been specially recruited and specially trained in the Welsh manner of fighting not just in the traditional methods of English warfare. Even the Romans had had to adapt to the terrain of Wales, and abandon the idea of looking the foe in the eye in a pitched battle. Earl Harold armed his men in the Welsh fashion, and they were trained to fight in mountain and river territory, to be able to follow and overcome the Welsh on their own ground.

In addition, Harold had spent careful months of preparation secretly sowing trouble amongst the warring princes in Wales. There was already a history of mistrust and suspicion — half the princes spent their time squabbling between themselves, trying to seize lands that belonged to other people, or on occasion, killing their relatives in order to inherit. Harold had spent some time stirring up discontent and dissent in an expert fashion, with the result that when war did come, Gruffudd was by no means certain of whom he could trust — or indeed, whether he could trust anybody.

The tactics of Earl Harold — which were in evidence later just before Harold's defeat at the Battle of Hastings, — were to attack unexpectedly after making long forced marches, confusing the enemy and catching him off guard. Right from the start, his campaign against Gruffudd was bewilderingly brilliant and effective.

Harold made his headquarters at Gloucester, and seemed about to make an attack on the south. The fact that his fleet was attacking the coast from Bristol seemed to back this up. But suddenly, much to Gruffudd's consternation, he found Harold's troops were in the north, penetrating into Gwynedd so that his home in Rhuddlan was threatened and he could barely reach his ship to escape them.

Harold's new plan for a spring offensive was that he himself would lead the forces of Wessex along the south coast from Bristol, while an army of Northumbrians under his brother and ally Earl Tostig would menace Gwynedd in the north. Gruffudd was driven back into Snowdonia and there was little he could do except bide his time and wait for Harold to withdraw, so that he could attack him as he retreated.

But all through the hot summer, Harold's armies continued their carnage and their savagery. The Welsh complained bitterly to each other that their lord must be a coward to skulk in the mountains saving his own skin while his lands ran with blood and his people suffered at the hands of the English.

The astute Earl Harold had announced a price on Gruffudd's head. A reward of 300 cattle would be paid. And when this noble warrior at last fell, it was not to his enemy, who might have granted him full battle honours. It was to his own men, who treacherously killed him and hacked off his head to take to Harold as a peace-offering. What is even more incredible is that the Earl of Wessex promptly married the lovely Eadgyth, Gruffudd's widow, and gave his fallen foe's half-brothers, Bleddyn and Rhiwallon, overlordship of Wales.

But Harold himself did not survive his Welsh foe for very long. Within months, he was confronting the Norman Duke William on the battlefield at Hastings, and the whole pattern of Welsh history as well as English history, was to change dramatically.

The Hall of Cynddylan

This famous lament was written in the ninth century by an unknown Welsh author. The warrior hero of the poem, Cynddylan, is thought to have been a nobleman from Powys who was killed by the invading Saxons in the sixth century, his court at Pengwern (now Shrewsbury) was destroyed and his lands were occupied.

The Hall in Darkness

"The Hall of Cynddylan's dark to-night:
The hearth is cold that burnt so bright:
My tears fall down in the ashes white.

The Hall of Cynddylan is dark to-night:
Without cheer of fire or candlelight;
None there, save God! Lord keep me aright!

Dark, dark, to-night is Cynddylan's Hall,
Where once the red fire-light cheered the wall:
The silence creeps and spreads o'er all.

The door of Cynddylan swings wide to-night
In the wind, on Carreg Hetwyth's height:
Its guests are gone, in its dark despite.

The hall of Cynddylan is bitter chill:
Where my harp had honour, the wind is shrill,
Where the guests once gathered on Hetwyth hill.

Ah, Hall of Cynddylan, it pierces me,
Where once was thy hearth's warm courtesy,
To-night thy sombre walls to see."

Chapter Five

WARRIOR PRINCESSES

Imagine a princess of dazzling beauty, daughter of Gruffudd ap Cynan, Lord of North Wales, wife of the South Wales prince Gruffudd ap Rhys ap Tudur: this was Gwenllian, who was to become celebrated in Welsh folk-history as 'The gallant Gwenllian who battle till death.'

There are few women leaders or warriors in the history of Wales, though we can be certain that, if those wild-haired women who defied the Romans on the shores of Anglesey were anything to go by, the warriors of Wales were always energetically backed up by their women, who were never noted for retiring, delicate habits.

The Welsh women were great beauties but they had spirit too, and alongside the great battles to preserve and unify Wales itself, there were many smaller conflicts where the love-lorn suitor attempted to capture the girl of his choice. But as this book is concerned with military battles, we will be hearing of two women who actually led their troops in the field. One was the Princess Gwenllian, who in the twelfth century went into battle with her two sons, in the absence of her husband. The other was one of the adversaries against whom the Welsh had to defend themselves — Aethelflaed, the daughter of Alfred the Great, who married Aethelred of Mercia, and who was known as 'the Lady of the Mercians'.

As well as keeping the Danes away from the Mercian boundaries, Aethelflaed held her kingdom against the Welsh, and even marched on Wales itself. She probably led attacks in various parts of Wales, but the most interesting of her victories — and possibly one of the most unusual battles ever fought in Wales — was the attack on the community at Llangorse, which is inextricably bound with one of the legends of Wales, that of a sunken city.

Tradition has it that land beneath Llangorse Lake belonged to a greedy princess who agree to marry the poor man who loved her if only he would give her — somehow — a fortune. So he murdered a rich merchant, and handed over the merchant's wealth to the princess, who was delighted. Neither of them turned a hair when the murdered man's ghost appeared to pronounce that doom would fall on the ninth generation of their descendants, and they lived on until the ninth generation was actually born. One night, there was a terrible flood in the hills around, and water surged across the land to drown the wicked princess and her husband, and all the people who lived there. So the lake was formed, according to the legend, and it is said that the mournful sound of sunken church bells can still be heard across the water.

In fact, there is no city of the type we would imagine beneath the lake, but recent archaeological evidence has endorsed the claim made in Victorian times that an early mediaeval artificial island existed in the lake. This was called a crannog, and some remains of a sort of stony mound about forty metres wide, with evidence of planking and wattle, has been identified. It was, say the experts, probably a palace built around the end of the ninth century, on an artificial island made of thousands of cubic feet of rock.

Though crannogs do exist in Ireland as the sites of royal palaces, there are no others in Wales, and it has been suggested that this was the palace of the Kings of Brycheiniog, who from the sixth century onwards, could claim Irish ancestry. But what has this to do with the Lady of the Mercians? Well, it was here that Aethelflaed made her appearance in 916 when her army attacked the island, took 34 people prisoner including the wife of 'the king', and destroyed the palace. So it was not the curse of a murdered merchant or the floods of legend which destroyed this palace in a lake, but the armies of Aethelflaed of Mercia, the fire and swords of her warriors.

The record in the *Anglo-Saxon Chronicle* does not give us much detail about the battle, and we have to imagine the Mercian troops gathered on the shore to storm the island, possibly succeeding as the day was dying. The flames of their torches would have streamed in the wind, while the women and old men who were within the palace tried desperately to save themselves. When the prisoners, screaming and lamenting, had been dragged away, the warriors fired the wooden buildings in earnest, and the island burned like a gigantic sun going down into the lake, its reflection eventually quenching the fires.

In the same legendary manner as the Lady of the Mercians leading her armies in the fateful raid on Llangorse Lake, the Princess Gwenllian haunts the folk-memory of Wales in her royal arms and trappings. Her sons, two royal princes, were at her side, and a huge force was at her back.

Some two hundred years separated Aethelflaed and Gwenllian and in that time, there had been many changes in Wales. By the time of the Battle of Hastings, the whole island of Britain had been in a more stable position, relatively, than it had ever been. Harold of Wessex had managed to unite most of the great English kingdoms and also to establish — by one means or another — reasonable relations with the kingdoms of the north and with Wales. He had built up the skill of his armies so that they were more than a match for the great Viking force which met him at Stamford Bridge.

But within the space of a day in 1066 on the battlefield of Hastings, all this was wiped out. The new monarch, William of Normandy, had his own ideas about the methods he intended to use to keep his hard-won kingdom under his control. He brought a fresh approach to gaining and keeping the loyalty of his subjects by granting land to his barons, who kept the peace in the surrounding areas, but were answerable to him so that the central power remained firmly in his hands. His favourites were as ruthless as he was himself in their ways of dealing with revolt, rebellion or protest, and the whole country soon began to groan beneath the heel of Norman domination.

It was at this time that William established the much-hated Marcher lordships along the frontier with Wales, and produced his own men, the 'Marcher lords' whose names were to become a byword for treachery. Hugh Lupus (Hugh the Wolf), Earl of Chester; Roger of Montgomery at Shrewsbury and William FitzOsbern in Hereford took it as their duty to hold the border against the Welsh, and to carry that border as far into Wales as they could in an attempt to conquer the country in the name of the new king.

It was not long before the simmering hatred of the conquered kingdom burst into flame, and there were rebellions against William in England within months of his victory at Hastings. He subdued these with the utmost brutality, and left parts of England almost devastated. The Welsh attempted to revolt, but they had their own internal struggles to contend with as well as keeping the all-powerful Normans at bay and the revolt died out before the year 1070 had dawned.

The types of battles which were now being fought, and the sort of weapons which were used inevitably began to change after the Norman conquest. In early Anglo-Saxon times, the various Welsh armies were composed mainly of archers and spearmen, who fought largely on foot. A few warriors rode hill ponies.

In many ways, the tactics they used were similar to the tactics used by the Romans. They would make a quick attack, then retreat just as rapidly, repeating this manoevre over and over. The Welsh were generally very lightly armed, in contrast to heavy trappings and

41

weapons which might have been used by their enemies, but this suited their style of fighting. Experts tell us that the Welsh archers could shoot quickly as they attacked and also as they retreated.

The Welsh became known as superb bowmen, and we will be hearing later of their exploits beyond the borders of Wales when their reputation spread through the whole of Europe and the western world.

The scene was soon set in Wales for an era of castle-building. The Romans were possibly the first to set up their own fortified buildings as bases for their efforts to subdue the native tribes. Each later conquerer or invader was to set up some sort of fortress or castle from which to hold lands that had been conquered, or to establish his own rule in another's territory. The castles of Wales, sadly ruined as most of them are today, tell the story of Welsh history.

Strongholds of the native Welsh princes can be seen at Dolbadarn, Ewloe and Dolwyddelan for example, while in the years after the Norman Conquest rose the great Norman castles such as Pembroke, Rhuddlan, Monmouth and Chepstow, which was built by the Marcher lord William FitzOsbern, Earl of Hereford. He managed to subdue practically the whole of Gwent before he died.

Quite a lot of the subjugation and appropriation of Wales was achieved not by fighting and battles, but through agreements, treaties and even marriage with the Norman overlords. In fact, the Welsh princes continued to fight between each other in exactly the same way as they had done previously, and some of the fiercest battles at this time took place between Welsh armies rather than Welsh versus Norman or versus some other foe. It was of course only to be expected that, as Harold had done, the Normans soon decided that the best way to have any effect on Wales was to interfere in internal politics and stir up trouble between the differing factions within Wales itself.

There had already been a number of battles since the Norman conquest, but largely between the warring factions within Wales. At a terrible encounter at Mechen, the two sons of Gruffudd ap Llywelyn were killed by the forces of their uncle, Gruffudd's brother Bleddyn, who seized control of Powys and Gwynedd.

Bleddyn's brother, Rhiwallon, fell in the same battle, leaving Bleddyn — who was apparently popular because he was gentle and good-natured — to carry on the tradition of his great brother Gruffudd ap Llywelyn and fight to unite and defend Wales. He tried hard, and allied himself with Mercia as Gruffudd had done, in an effort to keep the Normans from pressing across the border. In 1070, William the

Conqueror advanced on Chester, which fell leaving the road open into Wales. And the concerted efforts of his Marcher barons meant that the Welsh were never to be free from the threat of Norman invasion and slaughter.

But it was not Bleddyn who was to stop the Norman advance into Wales. He fell in 1077 when some of the Welsh chieftains, led by Rhys ab Owain, rebelled against his rule, and after a struggle the throne of Gwynedd was taken by his nephew Cynwrig. But Cynwrig was not the man his uncle had been — nor was he a match for a new claimant who was to appear, in the most dramatic manner, on the Welsh horizon. This newcomer was to prove yet another of the great Welsh heroes. His name was Gruffudd ap Cynan, and our heroine of this chapter, the Princess Gwenllian, was to be his daughter.

Gruffudd had spent his early years as an exile in Ireland. On the death of Bleddyn, he appeared with an Irish army at Deganwy, proclaiming his descent from the royal line of Gwynedd and demanding that the people should grant him the throne which was his rightful due. Never mind that King Cynwrig was already rather shakily settled in Gwynedd, Gruffudd, backed by his red-shirted men would not settle for anything less than the crown.

The people were reluctant to throw out their monarch for the benefit of a complete stranger, and Gruffudd did not wait. He sailed from Deganwy to Rhuddlan where he approached the Marcher lord Robert of Rhuddlan. Robert, a man steeped in cruelty and cunning, gave Gruffudd some soldiers but would not commit himself further, though it is said that an old servant of the great Gruffudd ap Llywelyn recognised that here was the man destined to be king of Wales, and presented the newcomer with the faded tunic of Gruffudd ap Llywelyn as a token.

His army swelled by men from Anglesey, Gruffudd returned to Deganwy and his forces met those of Cynwrig on a battlefield which is not known. In bitter conflict, the unfortunate monarch of Gwynedd fell in battle, leaving Gruffudd to advance through the kingdom he had won for himself. Cynwrig's cousin attempted to challenge the upstart and there was another battle — once again the site is not known — which was afterwards said to have taken place at 'the Bloody Acre'.

Robert of Rhuddlan made it clear that he expected to share in Gruffudd's triumph, but much to his chagrin, the new king of Gwynedd refused to share anything with a Norman overlord. Robert sulkily withdrew with his forces to await events, and it was not long before Gruffudd's men — an uneasy mixture of Irish and Viking — clashed with the citizens of Gwynedd.

Cynwrig's cousin, who had been defeated at the 'Bloody Acre', arrived to lead the rebellion and Gruffudd defended his position in battle at Bron yr Erw. Legend recounts what a magnificent figure he made, mounted on horseback amid his men, his sword flashing in his hand as he cut down his enemies. But in the end, he was lucky to escape the battlefield alive and was forced to return to the Ireland of his early years to gather his forces again.

He made a triumphant return with a fleet of thirty vessels, but since most of his warriors, in the Norse tradition, regarded looting and pillaging as a natural part of the spoils of war, they did not take kindly to his attempts to stop them indulging themselves, and he was forced to return to Ireland. Seeing that Gwynedd was in a state of confusion and largely undefended, Robert of Rhuddlan and Hugh Lupus chose this moment to advance into North Wales and lay it waste. They marched as far as Deganwy, grinding the countryside beneath the Norman heel and leaving smoking ruin behind them.

Gruffudd, once again in exile while Cynwrig's cousin assumed the title of king in Gwynedd, found an ally in the fugitive heir to Deheubarth, Rhys ap Tudur. Rhys ap Tudur too was descended from the royal line of Rhodri Mawr, but had been forced into exile in Brittany. Together, he and Gruffudd marched against Cynwrig's cousin in an effort to gain each of their kingdoms and restore the true line of kings to the kingdoms of Wales.

A great battle took place somewhere in south Ceredigion in 1079. It was called the Battle of Mynydd Carn, and seemingly broke all records since it did not come to an end within a day, as most battles at that time did. 'The moon rose on the hard-fought battle-field,' we are told by Professor Owen M. Edwards, 'throughout the night and the morrow was the beaten army pursued.'

Gruffudd's men must have made an interesting sight too since they were wielding long Irish spears on the one hand and double-edged Viking battle-axes on the other. This might even help to explain why their opponents were driven back — it could have been partly terror at the mere sight of the warriors who faced them. And as usual, Gruffudd himself rode into Welsh legend again in this battle as valorous beyond all imagining. However, whatever the reason, he won the day. The usurping cousin of Cynwrig fell on the field and at long last Gruffudd could feel he was safely established in his kingdom.

But both Gruffudd and Rhys ap Tudur had many battles still to fight, even though they were now undisputed lords in their own lands. These were against the Norman invaders, who pressed ever harder to extend their territories to the west. Rhys found that, after William the Conqueror decided to make a pilgrimage to St David's — apparently from the most pious motives, though we cannot be certain of this — there was a good deal of rebellion in the territory through which the English king had passed. He had to put down revolts in Dyfed and also to subdue smaller chiefs who rose against him.

Just as he seemed to have put his own house in order he was forced to march against the Norman lord Bernard de Neufmarche, who was busy with a programme of castle building that was intended to carve out a chunk of Welsh territory for himself. De Neufmarche had built a castle at Talgarth and in about 1091 he started work on one at Brecon. Rhys ap Tudur marched against him and in the battle that ensued, he was killed. His body, so we are told, was taken to St David's.

Gruffudd too seemed to be dogged by ill luck. The mighty warrior was brought down not by force of arms but by treachery. He was invited to attend a meeting of some rebellious chieftains and once in the Vale of Edeyrnion, was betrayed to the Norman barons of Chester and Shrewsbury. Captured by trickery at a 'peace' summit near Corwen, he was carried to Chester and thrown into prison.

Between Welshman and Norman, we can be sure there were many arguments, squabbles, even fights. But it was by building their castles that the Norman barons set their seal on the land and brought their language, their customs their ways to subtly transform the life and the landscape in Wales. However as we have seen, the Welsh have always fought to keep out the invader and to preserve their own existence as a nation. In spite of the castles and the authority of the Normans, they did not allow themselves to lose their identity, singly or collectively. Instead, as they had always done, they fought to keep their own character, language and way of life, their own heritage and their own visions.

To them, the Normans were always the enemy. At the beginning of the twelfth century, the Welsh might not have been able to attack their hated Norman foes in open battle, since their princes were no longer there to lead them, but still the Normans were always aware that if they ventured abroad at night, or tried to make their way through a dark wood with too few retainers, it was highly likely that they would be ambushed or attacked. Never did Wales become a voluntary part of the kingdom ruled by William the Conqueror and the Norman barons.

Gruffudd ap Cynan was rescued from prison in a most spectacular manner. We are told that a Welshman from Edeyrnion went to trade in Chester and while there, saw his lord in chains, presumably also thin and gaunt. The guards were drunk so without further ado, this devoted man picked up his king, threw him over one shoulder and carried him out, chains and all. And Gruffudd did not disappoint the followers who, like the honest man who had rescued him from prison, hope he would restore Wales to her former glory.

He began by waging guerilla war from Snowdonia, then went across to Ireland to gather a fleet of twenty-three ships and an army. He captured Anglesey from the Normans after some fierce fighting, so that the island was free again. Then he moved in on the treacherous Robert of Rhuddlan and managed to capture and kill his Norman foe. The rebellion spread throughout Wales, and intensified in savagery after the death of William the Conqueror. The new monarch, William Rufus, was even more violently hated and there were many scenes of bitter fighting at the close of the eleventh century between Welshman and Norman.

The soil of Wales was at this time nothing but a killing ground, and the Normans blinded, castrated and hanged any Welsh rebels who were unfortunate enough to fall into their hands. We can be certain that the Welsh retaliated with equal vigour. But eventually, Gruffudd and the lesser princes came to a sort of unspoken agreement with the Marcher barons, and the frontier of Wales, roughly as defined by Offa's Dyke, was accepted as marking the division between lands which the Normans could claim as their own, and lands which belonged to the Welsh, though there had been some Norman penetration into the south and there was also a Flemish settlement in south-west Wales. But Gruffudd was able to turn his attention to his kingdom and try to build up its prosperity.

This great hero king of Wales died in 1137, and was described by a chronicler as 'sovereign and protector and peacemaker of all Wales'. After an early career as a guerilla and mercenary leader, he had concentrated on unifying and strenghtening his kingdom and attempting to protect it from outside and internal enemies. Careful alliances as well as military force had protected Gwynedd, and by the time Gruffudd at last met his end, there was more security and peace in his territory than had been enjoyed for years.

One of his great allies in the last years of his life was Gruffudd ap

Rhys of Deheubarth, who married Gruffudd's daughter the Princess Gwenllian, and thus became his son-in-law. By a strange twist of fate both Gruffudd and the Lord of Deheubarth died in the same year, but two years earlier, on the death of King Henry I of England, the Princess Gwenllian had stepped onto the stage of history in the mailed coat of a soldier, to prove herself Wales' most noted heroine in battle.

In an effort to wage war afresh on the Norman usurpers who were still challenging him even in his own kingdom, the Lord of Deheubarth departed for the north with his eldest son, to ask for assistance from his father-in-law Gruffudd. He was still away when news was brought to Gwenllian that English reinforcements for the depleted force of the Norman lord Maurice de Londres, at Kidwelly Castle, had landed on the coast of Glamorgan. Her husband had made no arrangements of the action to be taken if these troops should arrive, so rather than allow them to proceed from the coast to their destination, Gwenllian herself led out a force to intercept them, accompanied by her two younger sons, Maelgwn and Morgan.

'Mounted on one of the sturdy surefooted galloways, of which Gruffudd kept many ready at all times for such sudden emergencies, although not the most stately of warsteeds, yet the best species of cavalry which the country afforded, the gallant lady rode forth,' we are told by an admiring writer.

Her small army proceeded from the forest of Ystrad Tywi to Kidwelly, making many detours to avoid being seen. She intended to surprise the English forces, and led her men past the looming towers of Kidwelly Castle to a spot some two miles further on, where she called a halt at the foot of Mynydd y Garreg, with the River Gwendraeth flowing before them. Here she waited while scouts went out to ascertain the position of the English force. They returned with the news that the English had not yet reached Kidwelly Castle, but were on the march, and Gwenllian sent a large detachment to intercept them, while the rest remained with her.

Here, however, her plans went horribly wrong. The reinforcements, under the leadership of a Welsh traitor called Gruffudd ap Llywelyn, had not only managed to evade the troops she had sent to intercept them, but had followed a roundabout route to the heights of Mynydd y Garreg, and two days after she had taken up her position by the river, the full force of English burst over the top of the hill in a deadly attack. Simultaneously, Baron Maurice de Londres thundered from the castle at the head of his own men, so that Gwenllian and the remnants of her army were trapped.

Gwenllian personally led her forces against these overwhelming odds, and legend paints a gallant picture of this lovely princess, hair streaming beneath her helmet, sword in hand, encouraging her men by her own example as well as by her exhortations, even as her forces were cut to pieces around her. The end was inevitable. The battle did not last long, and Gwenllian saw her son Maelgwn slaughtered at her side while he was attempting to protect her. Most of the Welsh army fell before the might of the Norman numbers, and the rest were herded together as prisoners, Gwenllian among them suffering from a wound she had received.

The Baron de Londres, far from displaying any chivalric appreciation of a noble and courageous foe, and a woman at that, ordered that Gwenllian should be immediately executed. His order was carried out on the spot. While the Normans howled jeers and her stricken son Morgan watched in horror, accompanied by the other Welsh captives, Baron de Londres and his crony, the renegade Gruffudd ap Llywelyn, gloated over the downfall of their wretched foe. Gwenllian's head was hacked from her body — but she had earned herself by her gallantry and courage, a unique place in Welsh history.

This old song was sung when the warrior princess was a baby in her father's court. "Sleep on" says the song, while Gruffudd ap Cynan was fighting the Normans. Her turn to carry on the struggle would arrive all too soon.

Sleep, Gwenllian

Sleep, Gwenllian, my heart's delight
Sleep on thro' shiv'ring spear and brand,
An apple rosy red within thy baby hand;
Thy pillowed cheeks a pair of roses bright,
Thy heart as happy day and night!
Mid all our woe, O! vision rare!
Sweet little princess cradled there,
Thy apple in thy hand thy all of earthly care.

Thy brethren battle with the foe,
Thy Sire's red strokes around him sweep,
Whilst thou, his bonny babe, art smiling through thy sleep.
All Gwalia shudders at the Norman blow!
What are the angels whispering low
Of thy father now?
Bright babe, asleep upon my knee,
How many a Queen of high degree
Would cast away her crown to slumber thus like thee!

Traditional Welsh Song

Chapter Six

THE BATTLES OF OWAIN GWYNEDD

Above the smiling Vale of Edeyrnion in North Wales rise the rugged heights of the Berwyn mountains. Here the real Wild Wales, which is often difficult to find, shows itself. Almost every inch of this area is drenched in blood, from the so-called Glyndŵr's Mount, where the last Lord of Glyndyfrdwy, Owain Glyndŵr, had a residence to the spot where Saint Garmon led his triumphant band of Welshmen against the Picts and Saxons in the celebrated 'Alleluia Victory'.

But one of the most dramatic conflicts to take place in this area was in August 1165, when the English King Henry II, at the head of an impressive army of 'the chosen warriors of England, Normandy, Flanders, Anjou, Gascony and all Scotland' made an attempt to subdue North Wales.

The whole of Wales had gathered at Corwen under the strong leadership of probably the most successful of all the Welsh princes — Owain Gwynedd. Here a large, determined army was ready to defend its country against the invading foe. As Henry's men advanced along the wooded Ceiriog Valley beneath their banners, the sky darkened ominously. The horses were restless, and the men eyed each other in the yellowish light with its sulphuric tang of anticipation. Flesh crawled. Colours were drained from rock, hill and tree. The earth was gathered, waiting . . .

Owain Gwynedd was the son of the Welsh leader Gruffudd ap Cynan; and the gallant princess Gwenllian who 'fought to the death in the cause of her people', was his sister. We have seen how at the time of Gwenllian's death, the Welsh princes were in constant battle with the Norman overlords. Gruffudd ap Cynan had fought to establish himself in Gwynedd, and Gwenllian's husband, Gruffudd ap Rhys of Deheubarth was only one of the South Wales princes to ally himself with the great prince of the North.

Already, before Gwenllian's murder, the princes were making attempts to join their forces. Afterwards, when she became a national heroine whose very name was taken up as a war-cry, so that the Welsh shouted 'Maes Gwenllian' as they went into battle, the princes gathered their forces with renewed determination and the whole of

Wales threw its weight against the much-hated Normans in an attempt to drive them out of the country, particularly out of South Wales where they were strongest.

Castles were attacked, and when the Earl of Chester advanced into Wales, the records tell us that 'it was with difficulty that he himself, with five only of his soldiers were able to escape; the rest of his forces having been put to the sword.' This says a great deal for the freshly embittered feelings of the Welsh, who would not have hesitated to put the whole lot of Norman lords and their hangers-on to the sword if they had had the opportunity. The fact that a handful of the English got away would suggest they were very lucky.

The Normans were invaders who had stolen the land that made them fat, and turned the rightful owners into serfs and slaves. So far as most of the Welsh were concerned, there could never be peace, far less peaceful integration.

One day, they told each other, there would be retribution. And the day of reckoning seemed to have come when, towards the end of 1136, Gruffudd ap Cynan's sons, Owain Gwynedd and his brother Cadwaladr marched into South Wales at the head of an army which consisted, so we are told, of six thousand infantry and two thousand horse, all of whom were clad in armour and completely armed. This in itself must have been a sight to marvel at, as the Welsh generally avoided heavy arms.

'Having excited Gruffudd ap Rhys and several chieftains in South Wales to join them, with considerable supplies,' we are told, 'they subdued the whole country, as far as Cardigan, expelling the foreigners, and replacing the native inhabitants.'

The Normans, regarding this as dangerous total war, advanced to put down the insurrection. Led again by the Earl of Chester, a formidable force of Normans, Flemings and English, under the command of several powerful barons, met the Welsh troops on the northern side of the Teifi near Cardigan. There are few details of this battle, except that the conflict was bloody and terrible, and that the English lost three thousand men. Defeated, they tried to escape to the shelter of their own castles, and the victorious Welsh, pressing them hard, took large numbers of prisoners. It is even reported that some of the prisoners were taken and guarded by Welsh women, behind the lines, so thoroughly were the English defeated and demoralised.

As the English scrambled in retreat to the bridge across the Teifi, many of their soldiers fell into the river and were drowned. The bridge itself — apparently because of the huge weight of men attempting to cross it — chose this inauspicious moment to collapse, throwing masses of bodies to perish among the corpses already in the water. For the English it must indeed have been a black and bitter day. The enraged Welsh then proceeded to repossess themselves of the lands around on which the Normans had built castles, which they considered theirs by right, of which they had been robbed.

The battles of Owain Gwynedd were being fought, as it were, even before the death of his father. Owain and his brother Cadwaladr rode out to lead the Welsh forces together just as they did at this great Welsh victory at Cardigan. Both were skilled soldiers but whereas Owain, like his father, could see the advantages in peace and caution, Cadwaladr had no time for anything but military glory.

Owain would have been happy to pursue the settled and peaceful policies which Gruffudd (who died in the year following the battle at Cardigan) had planned for his kingdom. His ambition was to strengthen the alliances of Gwynedd and assist her to further prosperity. But Cadwaladr chose to see their father's achievements in the light of his great victories, and wanted more victory, particularly over the English who were weakened at this time by their own struggle between the claims of Stephen and Matilda for the throne.

The civil war in England meant that there was little or no interference in Welsh affairs from the centre of English government during this period. But the border and Marcher lords were free to wage their own wars on Wales as they chose, while the Welsh in their turn were free to try and get their internal affairs organised. Gruffudd's sons, Owain Gwynedd and Cadwaladr, seemed at first to be working together for the unity of their own kingdom and for the whole of Wales, and it appeared as though Gruffudd's dream of a united country would be fulfilled.

What smashed this dream, however, and set Owain's reluctant feet onto a path of war and conflict, was when in 1143, the lord of Deheubarth's son, Anarawd, was on the point of marrying Owain's daughter. This would have united the kingdoms of Deheubarth and Gwynedd in the same way that Gwenllian's marriage had done, and would have strengthened Welsh unity.

The reckless and unthinking Prince Cadwaladr took it into his head, however, to kill Anarawd in a dispute over boundaries — one of the most fiercely charged subjects among the Welsh.

His foolish and grievous act, ill-considered in all respects and one which could in no way be justified, roused bitter anger in the south, where young Anarawd was regarded as 'the hope and the strength and the glory of the men of the south'. In the north, Owain's court was filled with grief, both for his sorrowing and shocked daughter, who had lost her bridegroom on the eve of their marriage, and for the fact that Cadwaladr could have allowed himself to do such a thing.

Owain had to decide whether to let his policies of peace and unity go — possibly for good — and to side with his brother in violence against the outrage of the south and the rest of Wales; or whether to take action against Cadwaladr in order to save his dreams of a united country.

In spite of the fact that until then, he and his brother had been very close and had had implicit trust in each other's judgement, Owain chose the latter course. He sent his sons with troops to Cadwaladr's castle at Aberystwyth, to burn it and seize his brother's lands.

Cadwaladr, a dramatic and colourful exile, responded in time-honoured fashion by trying to bring down the brother he had once loved. He sailed into the Menai Straits at the head of a fleet of pirates, but even though he changed his mind about fighting Owain, and was tearfully reunited with him, it was not surprising that after this, he was regarded as no fit person to be trusted with Owain's confidence.

Down in the south, Cadwaladr was openly referred to as a murderer, and the people of Anglesey made their feelings even clearer. They drove him from the island, with shrieks of 'Murderer!' and 'Traitor!' In the typical manner of such 'black sheep', he immediately took to conniving with the hated Normans to try and get even with his brother.

The Normans were quick to see the advantages of splitting the loyalties of north and south, and setting one brother against another. They marched against Wales and against Owain. The wars which he had hoped to avoid were now to continue intermittently until his death.

More important to him than the news of sieges, battles, the victories and the losses of his sons and the sons of Gruffudd ap Rhys of Deheubarth as they led the armies of the princes against those of the Marcher barons was the news of the death of his favourite son, Rhun.

'The whole country,' says Owen M. Edwards, 'grieved with the stricken father for the popular young prince, whose blue, laughing eyes and golden curly hair are described by the chronicler, as well as his kindly wisdom in peace and courage in battle. His people thought that Owain Gwynedd would die of a broken heart, and feared that God would leave their country as a tempest-tossed rudderless vessel.'

It was the long siege of Mold — the key to the heartlands of the north, which was in Norman hands — that eventually roused Owain to fight on and to try once again to achieve the vision of peace and unity his father had bequeathed to him. In 1146, the castle at Mold fell to the Welsh; the princes continued to strengthen their borders and extended them. By 1152, Owain knew that if the princes continued to accept his leadership and ally themselves together, they could hold the country, and they could stand up to any attacks they might be subjected to.

On the whole, Owain Gwynedd had thus more or less succeeded in his dream to bring a relative peace to the whole of Wales, and had driven his brother and the Normans beyond the borders, when the circumstances altered significantly. A new king succeeded to the throne of England.

Henry II had one aim in view when he looked to the west — to crush the might of his far-too-powerful Marcher barons. He was not really concerned with making war on the Welsh for their own sake, but there were two reasons why he considered it essential to defeat Owain Gwynedd and the other princes. The whole system of marcher lordships had been brought into being so that the Marcher lords, acting on behalf of the crown, could keep the Welsh in check. Their whole existence, their ability to control and keep order in the surrounding areas, rested on the fact that they had to be strong, they had to have forces at their disposal.

Even alone, King Henry considered, they were too much of a threat to his authority. But if they should proceed to ally themselves with the Welsh — with Owain and the other princes — the combined force would be formidable. No, there was nothing else for it. In order to get rid of the barons, Owain Gwynedd and his armies had to go first.

Consequently, Henry mounted a campaign to subdue Wales and the Welsh. His army set off from Chester along the coast to Rhuddlan, while a fleet sailed ahead to Anglesey. He tried to take Owain by surprise from the rear by leading a small force himself to harrass Owain's army, which was at Basingstoke. Instead of causing havoc, however, he found that Owain's sons were ready for him. He was ambushed, and we are told that Henry of Essex, who was carrying the royal banner, threw it away in panic as he fled from the scene. King Henry's force suffered heavy losses, and he himself was lucky to escape alive.

Owain slowly retreated, not accepting a pitched battle but following the same tactics the Welsh had always used — of harrassing the English armies in guerilla raids while skilfully avoiding direct combat. Once again, the Welsh used the cover of trees and woods while the English armies were forced to keep to the sandy coastal area that made for difficult marching. They might have been following in the footsteps of the Roman legionaires who had passed along this same coast with the Roman eagles a thousand years before.

At Rhuddlan, Henry considered the situation, and what might have happened next is anybody's guess, except that news reached Henry of the destruction of the fleet he had sent to Anglesey. The ships had landed, and the men aboard had begun to loot the churches — probably the only places where they might have found anything of value. There were no troops to repel them, but the people of Anglesey — who must have been tired of scenes like this — threw themselves in outraged fury on the invaders at Tal-y-Moelfre.

The shaken troops tried to return to their ships, but most of them never made it. The battle continued in the water, turning the sea red. The people of Anglesey had learned how to kill — they had had to over the years in order to survive. According to Welsh legend, the waters of the Menai Straits did not ebb on that day, such was the flow of blood spilled in the battle. Among those who perished was Henry's bastard uncle, whose mother had been the Welsh Princess Nest of Deheubarth. As a young girl, Nest had spent some time at the English court, where she had had a passionate liaison with the English King Henry I.

Owain and Henry both felt it expedient to make peace, and the other Welsh princes also accepted the terms that were offered, though rather grudgingly. Owain's preference was always for diplomacy rather than fighting. But the princes were not satisfied, and when the peace had been made, it was not long before trouble broke out again. It was the same old story. The princes were fighting amongst themselves as well as against the Normans and the king. Borders were being fortified. There was widespread suspicion, castles were attacked, it was civil war.

Even Owain felt obliged to protect himself. He seized Cyfeiliog and Arwystli, strengthening his own borders, and also began diplomatic negotiations with the other princes, who had previously been suspicious and resentful of any attempt to ally themselves together. When matters reached such a dangerous state that Henry felt he could no longer allow Owain his freedom, but this time must put him down for good and all, the situation was very different to when Henry had first marched on Wales.

This time, in 1165, Owain and all the Welsh princes stood united, and the army that faced the English was a far greater force than the one which had shadowed the king along the North Wales coast, playing cat and mouse. Henry marched into Wales with his own army — the one which we have seen attempt to follow the Ceiriog Valley and then scale the heights of the Berwyn mountains. It was largely made up of mercenaries, tough fighting men from Anjou, Normandy, Gascony and Flanders.

Henry's aim was to cut through from Oswestry along the Ceiriog Valley, cross the Berwyn, and head for Snowdon. He wanted to break the Welsh by cutting their resistance in two.

From Corwen, Owain Gwynedd's best warriors went forward over the Berwyn to the upper Ceiriog valley which was an impenetrable forest in those days. Henry marched towards them with his foresters ahead, hacking a way through for his massive army. The foresters were guarded by the flower of Henry's army and by his pikemen. At Bron-y-garth, they were ambushed by the advance troops from the Welsh army. This was called the battle of Crogen and the Welsh hurled themselves with such fury on the English and displayed such fine fighting qualities that for many years after the battle the word among English soldiers for courage was "Crogen". Henry himself narrowly escaped with his life and he lost so many men that he was forced to retreat. In revenge, he had the eyes torn out of the heads of Owain Gwynedd's two sons whom he was holding as hostages.

Henry's army fled into the Berwyn mountains, raiding churches and destroying cemetries in its rage. Then, as by divine intervention, the heavens opened and a terrible storm broke upon Henry's tired army. Lashed unmercifully by torrential rain and hail, the almost drowned army was forced to retreat.

But the rout and retreat following the rain-lashed 'battle' of the Berwyn was not the only retreat Henry had to make. After their ignominious retreat, wet, tired and almost collapsing with hunger, he tried to persuade his armies to advance into Wales along the coast, but once again he was to be frustrated. He had trouble with his fleet, and Owain played a waiting game and stayed tantalisingly out of reach. The defeated Henry and his army withdrew for the last time from the conquest of Wales.

The Battle of Tal-y-Moelfre

I celebrate Rhodri's bounteous heir,
Border-land's guardian, rightful ruler,
Britain's true lord, trial-hardened Owain,
King who neither cringes nor covets.
Three legions came, sea-surge's vessels,
Three strong navies seeking to crush him.
One from Ireland, a second with soldiers
From the Norsemen, long prows of the deep,
And the third sailing from Normandy,
And the task for it dire and dreadful.
And Môn's dragon, savage his mood in war,
And clamour, bold their call for battle,
And before him a grim wild welter
And clash and havoc and tragic death,
Troop on bloodstained troop, throb on frightened throb,
At Tal-y-Moelfre a thousand war-cries,
Shaft on shining shaft, spear upon spear,
Fear on deep fear, drowing on drowning.
And no ebb in Menai from tides of blood,
And the stain of men's blood in the brine.
And grey armour and ruin's anguish,
And corpses heaped by a red-speared lord,
And England's horde and engagement with it
And them demolished in the shambles.
And the fame raised of a savage sword
In seven-score tongues to praise him long.

Gwalchmai ap Meilyr

Chapter Seven

BATTLES OF TWO ROYAL FAMILIES

There were, of course, fighting and feuds in every generation but some people and their doings seem more interesting, more colourful and more glamorous than the rest. One character from English history who is always painted larger-than-life is King John, who usually appears in legends garbed in black, presiding over the tortures being handed out by the Sheriff of Nottingham to the followers of Robin Hood.

In fact, though, King John had much closer links with Wales than he did with Nottingham. Owain Gwynedd's grandson Llywelyn ab Iorwerth, who is called Llywelyn Fawr (*Llywelyn the Great*), married King John's daughter Princess Joan, and was thus this evil monarch's son-in-law. But as with all families, great or lesser born, there are little squabbles and disagreements from time to time; it comes as no surprise to hear that Llywelyn and his royal in-law spent quite a lot of time at each other's throats.

The last effort of Henry II to subdue Owain Gwynedd and the Welsh left Owain free after the English had withdrawn, to recover the castles of Prestatyn, Basingstoke and Rhuddlan. But in the November of 1169, Owain died and was buried at Bangor. His brother Cadwaladr, who had been his evil genius, followed him in 1172 to share the same grave in Bangor Cathedral.

In the period following Owain's death, there is a distinctly different flavour to the stories which are told about the battles of the time. Many more of the characters who appear in them are Norman, or English who had settled in Wales. Just as in the tales of Robin Hood, the outlaw and his band were the embodiment of the 'yeomen of England' against the cruel might of monarchs who seemed to care little about the good of England and her people, so the heroes of Welsh legend at this time tried to redress wrongs and avenge crimes committed by their evil overlords against Wales and the Welsh.

One incident which dates from this period is that of the banquet of death planned by the cruel William de Braose at Abergavenny Castle in 1176. A group of Welsh chiefs from the surrounding area were invited to a 'peace conference', and they trustingly accepted the seemingly sincere invitation. Seisyll ap Dyfnwal, a near neighbour to the castle from Upper Gwent, was even accompanied by his small son Gruffudd. But as they sat at meat, the whole group including young Gruffudd was ruthlessly slaughtered.

Nor was this the end of the outrage which de Braose and his men perpetuated on the Welsh tribes. The homes of all the murdered chiefs were attacked and their families were killed without mercy, including the children. Since the concept of hospitality to a guest was one of the most sacred ideals in the Welsh code — and since this had been violently abused when the murders were committed as the guests sat at their host's table — the Welsh were outraged far beyond an ordinary incident of war.

The sons who had survived the murdered chiefs swore never to rest until they had avenged their fathers. The people of Gwent swore never to trust an Englishman again.

In the best legendary tradition, this band of Welsh avengers made several attempts to kill de Braose and his crony Ranulf Poer, Sheriff of Hereford, who had actually carried out the murders. They tried on one occasion to enter Abergavenny Castle by night over the battlements, but the murderers got away. Later, they stormed the half-finished walls of a new castle being built at Dingestow, and Ranulf Poer was practically beheaded with a sword when he was caught. A priest, conveniently nearby, was hurried to his side in time — just — to shrive him before he died.

William de Braose had fallen into a deep trench, and was being dragged from it to meet his end at the hands of the angry Welsh, when he was saved by his own men. But he was to receive a just fate later when King John, another evil man who had been a close crony, suddenly turned against him and left him eventually to die penniless in exile, while his wife and eldest child were thrown into Windsor Castle and allowed to starve to death.

But if this was the era of colourfully evil and wicked men, there were the heroes too, and the hero of Wales at the end of the twelfth century was the Lord of Deheubarth Rhys ap Gruffudd, who is usually referred to as 'the Lord Rhys'. Rhys had master-minded the recovery of much of the Vale of Tywi, as well as Dyfed and Ceredigion, and he had allied himself with Owain Gwynedd in Owain's fight against England. He had been with Owain at Crogen when the English King Henry II was being beaten back by the flower of the Welsh warriors and by those storms across the Berwyn.

Later, though, Rees made his peace with Henry. There was a dramatic meeting, so we are told, between King and lord as Henry was riding in South Wales, his hawk on his wrist. Each recognised they had something to gain from peaceful collaboration. Lord Rees gave Henry assistance when the king needed it to put down the revolts and rebellions of his turbulent barons; in return, Henry tactily approved and did not interfere with Rees' growing power in the south. 'The Lord Rees' was able to rule in immense power and splendour in his capacity as the English king's 'Justiciar of South Wales', and so long as he was at peace with Henry and had his support, he could make every attempt to unify his lands without fear of reprisals from a worried English crown. Moreover, none of the other Welsh princes dared to try and oppose him.

In the language of song and fable, the feuds and the vows and the pledges of this time come down to us like faded flowers, treasured relics of the past. The women were beautiful beyond believing, the men were god-like. Life was larger-than-life, every emotion was lived to its last drop, every action was filled with symbolism.

Of course, the reality was rather different. When Owain Gwynedd, whose skill at soldiery was matched with a genius at diplomacy, left the north without his protection on his death, his lands were inherited by his sons. In the usual course of events, they squabbled amongst themselves for the throne of Gwynedd, and in the process of the struggle, the work which Owain had tried to do for peace and unity was, as generally happened, sadly undermined. It was left to Owain's grandson Llywelyn, who was born at Dolwyddelan Castle in 1173, to pull the scattered pieces of what had been the kingdom of Gwynedd together.

He bided his time, and was twenty-one when he challenged the nominal prince of Gwynedd, his Uncle Dafydd, for his crown. The resulting Battle of Aberconwy, fought between Llywelyn and his uncle, was a victory for Llywelyn and his small army. His uncle, who lived afterwards in the hope that he would be able to win his kingdom back, removed beyond the borders of Wales into Shropshire, where he remained in exile, observing events. Llywelyn meantime set about strengthening his position in Gwynedd.

The days of peace between King Henry II and the Lord Rhys had gone, and there were young and ambitious princes jostling for power once again within the kingdoms of Wales. In England, the throne had been held during most of the reign of Richard I, by his brother who became King John of England.

Llywelyn has been called a great opportunist. He certainly displayed this characteristic now when he sought and won the hand of Princess Joan, John's bastard daughter, thus gaining the English king as a father-in-law. He was then able to benefit from John's support in his own struggle against the other Welsh princes.

With John's troops backing his own forces, Llywelyn proceeded to clear away the threat posed by Gwenwynwyn, Prince of Powys, who was trapped between Llywelyn's armies over-running Powys, and John's men in the east. Gwenwynwyn himself was taken prisoner by John in Shrewsbury.

Other princes fled, and Llywelyn revived the old alliance with the south by giving the sons of Rhys ap Gruffudd — the Lord Rhys — power in Ceredigion as his allies. He then went north and possessed himself of the castles of Deganwy, Rhuddlan, Mold and Holywell, which belonged to the Earl of Chester. By this time, however, he had made himself far too powerful for the liking of his father-in-law, King John, who would allow no-one to pose a possible threat to him, son-in-law or not.

As a result, King John turned against Llywelyn and began to assemble a huge army to invade Wales and destroy him. The other princes who had been forced to bend the knee to Llywelyn or who had fled from him, joined in this venture with enthusiasm, allying themselves with the English king. At his side when the combined force set out from Chester along the coastal plain, were the standards and banners of the Earl of Chester, whose castles were now in Llywelyn's hands, as well as those of Gwenwynwyn of Powys, whom John had restored to favour, and two of the sons of Rhys ap Gruffudd who saw more chance of grabbing land and power for themselves under the English king than they would achieve by helping their brothers in alliance with Llywelyn.

Just as dramatic as the invasion of North Wales by the great army of mercenaries under Henry II, which had been beaten back by stinging hail and lashing winds across the Berwyn, was the sight of King John of England and his ill-assorted and ungainly host as they advanced from Chester along the coast. John was an astute and clever strategist who could handle his troops, but he had counted without the brilliance of Llywelyn in using the same defensive tactics the Welsh had always used in this sort of situation.

The diplomatic skill and tact which had been such a characteristic of Owain Gwynedd was present in the character of his grandson, along with all the military flair and ability that had marked Owain's brother, the unfortunate Cadwaladr. Llywelyn knew he could not hope to defeat this enormous army, and rather than make the attempt, he had moved all his people, his flocks, all the food there was, to the security of the distant mountains, looming against the sky in the growing heat of the steadily-climbing summer sun.

The armies of King John and his allies met nothing but dry, bare, barren earth. As they pressed forward, the days grew hotter, and what few crops they managed to find were withered and dying. None of the few people the army encountered had anything of which they could be robbed, or which they might have given up under torture or bribes. Llywelyn had stripped the land bare in order to impede the progress of the army. As a result, food became more precious than gold. Soldiers and their commanders alike fought to pay a penny half-penny for a single egg, and even the flesh of their own horses, which they were forced to eat to save them from starvation, seemed like the most delicious of rare meats.

Frustrated, the king had no option but to retreat — but he returned again at the end of the summer, when the Welsh would have to leave the sanctuary of the mountains and see to their harvest and their crops, or else leave themselves with no food for the winter. The invading armies came prepared this time, and brought extra supplies of food. And they were driven by bitter anger enhanced by months of humiliated frustration.

They penetrated as far as Bangor, where they mercilessly ravaged the town and the cathedral. Citizens were killed, raped; the bishop, taking sanctuary in his church, was dragged out even as the building blazed around him, and John demanded a ransom for him of two hundred hawks.

The reports of how his kingdom was suffering devastation at the hands of this enormous and merciless horde drove Llywelyn into immediate action. He sent his wife as a mediator to her father, King John, with instructions to negotiate for peace on any terms.

Joan was a spirited lady of immense character but even with her tactful intervention, the price that had to be paid for peace almost crippled Llywelyn. John would take no less than twenty thousand head of cattle, and all the lands west of the River Conwy. He demanded similarly humiliating terms from Llywelyn's allies, the two sons of Rhys who had kept up the old alliance in the south.

John was determined that there should be no more emergence of the

Welsh — whichever prince or leader it might be — to power, and he allowed the barons to do more or less exactly as they liked after this, so long as they kept Wales down. This meant, however, that the outrages of villains like Faulkes de Breaute and Robert Vipont, barons whose names were thoroughly black even in this age of so many wicked barons, resulted in the Welsh uniting against their common enemies.

The Welsh princes who had allied themselves with John in the past turned instead to Llywelyn as the only man who could save them all. And even as they tried to unite, and as Llywelyn was able to consider himself the virtual prince of the whole of Wales, the nation at long last a complete kingdom, the dreams of those other great princes who had fought so hard for this very aim now wonderfully achieved, John's fear and fury grew. From the royal castles in Wales and the castles of the barons, the iron hand of cruelty and injustice came down harder than ever on the Welsh people.

These were dark days when, as Professor O.M. Edwards tells us: 'No bell had tolled in Wales for five years, the energy of the Cistercians had turned into spiritual paralysis, and the curse of the Church lay on the harried land.' But in 1212, Llywelyn sent messengers to the Pope, who pronounced that he and the other Welsh princes were freed from their oaths of allegiance to John. Backed by the Church, Llywelyn was able to try and rid Wales of the influence of the English king.

He took what might seem a strange step — but diplomacy can make for odd bedfellows. He threw in his lot with the English barons, and joined their alliance against the king, even though John was now making strong attempts to win his support back. When history was written on the island of Runnymede, and the Magna Carta was drawn up and signed, Llywelyn as well as the other barons had put forward his personal claims to have his interests and the interests of his people protected, and there were three clauses relating to Wales in the document.

Llywelyn arranged further alliances and close links with the powerful baronial families by marrying his children to a de Braose, a Mortimer and into the family of the Earl of Chester. Most of his later battles were not to be against these traditional foes, but against other Welsh princes, who in the age-honoured manner, continued to squabble between each other and against any prince who was more powerful than themselves. The concept of a united Wales, while difficult to achieve, proved — whenever it did show signs of being imminent — far more difficult to perpetuate.

King John had died in 1216, leaving as his heir the boy Henry III, who did not at first pose much of a threat to Llywelyn. In his later years, he spent most of his time attempting to act as an intermediary and champion between barons, crown and his own prices. The battles he fought were largely attacks on castles, or over-running the land of rebel princes to try and keep the peace. He made every attempt to keep his wars, so far as they could be kept, civilised. He did not approve of pillaging. Always, as his grandfather Owain Gwynedd had done, he preferred negotiations, diplomacy, tact, peaceful agreement. And by the time of his death in 1240, he had done more than any other Welsh prince to demonstrate the reality of a peaceful independence for Wales.

The slaughter of the saints.

The Romans murdering the druids of Anglesey.

King Arthur, a statue c.c. 1480
among the high kings of Europe at Innsbruck.

*The warriors of the Round Table — the legend of Arthur
probably rose from a band of Celtic fighting horsemen.*

An aerial view of the remains of Offa's Dyke,
for centuries the frontier between England and Wales.

A Celtic war chariot rebuilt from remains found on Anglesey.

Abergavenny castle where the Normans murdered Welsh Princes who attended a peace-making feast there.

*The sculpture which honours the
Welsh princes at Aberffraw, Anglesey.*

*Llywelyn ab Iorwerth's stone coffin which was moved from
Aberconwy Abbey and now rests in Llanrwst church.*

Dolwyddelan castle which held the western frontier of Gwynedd until 1283.

Dolbadarn castle among the northern mountains.

Castell y Bere, a Welsh castle in southern Snowdonia.

The stone at Cilmeri commemorates the place where Llywelyn ap Gruffudd was killed.

Owain Glyndŵr, a national leader with a national dream.

Harlech castle — one of the strongholds of Glyndŵr.

*Wales still salutes its heroes — this inn at Llanddona,
Anglesey, is one of the many which carries Glyndŵr's name.*

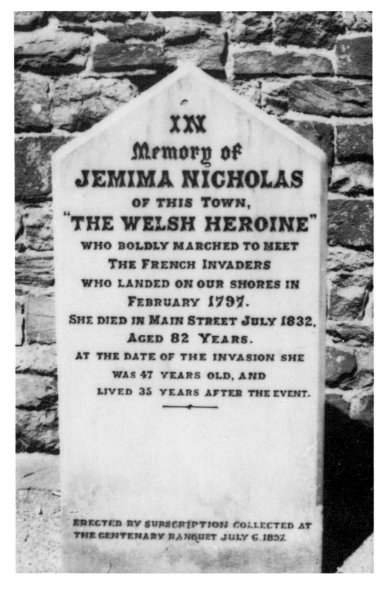

IN
Memory of
JEMIMA NICHOLAS
OF THIS TOWN,
"THE WELSH HEROINE"
WHO BOLDLY MARCHED TO MEET
THE FRENCH INVADERS
WHO LANDED ON OUR SHORES IN
FEBRUARY 1797.
SHE DIED IN MAIN STREET JULY 1832,
AGED 82 YEARS.
AT THE DATE OF THE INVASION SHE
WAS 47 YEARS OLD, AND
LIVED 35 YEARS AFTER THE EVENT.

ERECTED BY SUBSCRIPTION COLLECTED AT
THE CENTENARY BANQUET JULY 6.1897.

Jemima Nicholas' gravestone in Fishguard.

*The soldiers in the Westgate Hotel at Newport
opened fire on the Chartist crowd.*

A reminder, in Merthyr, of the death of Dic Penderyn.

An old print showing Rebecca in action.

An inn near Carmarthen still reminds us of the Rebecca Riots and the days when tollhouses were burnt.

In Praise of Llywelyn ab Iorwerth

Bold was Arthur once, and his men, spreading
    Anguish on every side,
    Soldiers' dearly loved soldier,
    As you are today, bold man.

Bold man, Llywelyn, most favoured his bards
    And his myriad men.
    Christendom's lord will not loose
    England's bonds, arrogant race.

Arrogant any not bound to my lord,
    Man who prizes not greed.
    God made not, heaven's high king,
    Nor will make, a man so good.

You have made war, Britain's mainstay, gold spear,
    No delight to your foes.
    To the Welsh, wrathful comrade,
    England's haven surrendered.

High tide's might, when at ease he is gentle,
    A generous ruler,
    Savage when he is close-pressed,
    Fearsome assault, fierce pursuit.

Unconcealed your assault, Llŷr's zeal and Brân's
    And red-stained your spear-shaft.
    There have you roved, lord of men,
    Through sword-strokes, royal eagle.

Since you have ruled, the Welsh uproot England,
    Seizing thousands of spoils,
    Dragon's wealth, fearsome ruler,
    Savage lord's horde, ill-gotten.

Llywelyn ap Llywarch

Chapter Eight

THE BATTLES OF LLYWELYN THE LAST

By traditional Welsh law, a man's possessions, including his lands, were divided equally on his death between all his sons. The kingdoms and princedoms could thus be weakened if there was no strong inheritor to keep and hold power for himself, and if all the relatives of the departed prince attempted to grab a piece of his inheritance for themselves.

By the end of the twelfth century, there had been so much in-fighting and splitting of the ancient kingdoms that Gwynedd in the north, alone remained the power it had once been. The rest of the kingdoms had largely disintegrated into tiny and petty princedoms or lordships.

The efforts of Llywelyn ab Iorwerth (*Llywelyn the Great*) to strengthen his own territories and to unite the other kingdoms into a nation, culminated in 1216 in a situation where he was able to make a treaty with the King of France and speak not only for his own kingdom of Gwynedd, but for the other Welsh rulers, who had accepted his overlordship. When in the same year he held a meeting of the princes at Aberdyfi, it is quite possible that a ceremony of fealty where the princes swore homage to him took place.

Llywelyn and the future princes of Gwynedd aimed that all other Welsh princes should be their vassals, and should do them homage. They in their turn would offer fealty on the behalf of the whole of Wales, to the King of England. Some of the more idealistic Welsh still thought in terms of complete independence for Wales, but times were changing and the more realistic saw that it would be fanciful to suppose that the demands of the English crown would suddenly disappear, or cease. It was not possible either to ignore England, disregard it or hope that it would go away.

But Llywelyn wanted recognition for himself and his heirs as the representative of all the other princes, who could on their behalf intervene as a virtual 'King' of Wales with any fellow King, as an equal. He planned and put into operation a great Council to protect the lesser princes. Any member could call for aid on the Council and its forces, so there was no chance of a hot-headed individual suddenly taking power and over-running the lands of his neighbour, which had of course happened many times in the past.

But this would have meant, of course, that Wales no longer consisted of various kingdoms, each with its own independent prince or king, who had power to proffer his own homage if he chose to do so. The subject princes would be reduced to a lesser status than the Prince of Gwynedd, and they would not have been able to negotiate directly with other rulers, only through the all-powerful Prince of Gwynedd.

What really rankled with these proud princes, was that the Prince of Gwynedd had no more right than they did to assume control and overlordship over the whole of Wales and the other kingdoms which were just as ancient and royal as his own. And so there was a great deal of resentment, and the concept of a united Wales never wholly worked.

Added to which, not all the Princes of Gwynedd were of the stature and vision of Llywelyn. After his death, his younger son Dafydd succeeded, in spite of the fact that there was an elder son, Gruffudd. Gruffudd had rebelled against his father over policy, and had been imprisoned by Llywelyn as a result. He had been a prisoner at Cricieth for six years before his father's death, and his brother Dafydd saw no reason to set him free, particularly as there was a great deal of support for him in Wales and in the marches.

Gruffudd favoured complete independence for Wales, while Dafydd was quite happy to accept the status of vassal-prince to the English King Henry III — for the time being, anyway. Henry decided to take advantage of this quarrel between the brothers, and advanced with an army to Chester, where Dafydd swore homage. Gruffudd was handed over with other Welsh hostages including his wife and sons, to be incarcerated in the Tower of London.

In legendary fashion, this hero of Welsh independence attempted to escape by climbing down a make-shift rope of tapestries and sheets from the top of the Tower. Spectacularly, it broke and he was killed in the resulting fall — appropriately enough, on St David's Day, 1244. His brother Dafydd realised that this martyr-like death would inflame the Welsh, and he decided to switch to Gruffudd's policy for independence and to ready his armies for war with Henry III.

Once again an invading force marched along the coast as far as Deganwy, and once again the Welsh kept their distance and made guerilla-type attacks, but would not join in a pitched battle. Two months dragged past as they sat the campaign out in their sprawling camps. The English ravaged far and wide, and hunger was stalking both forces but there had been no face-to-face fighting, and neither David nor Henry had achieved anything like a victory.

The battle which did ensue — and which was horrific — resulted not from any cunning strategy or surprise offensive. An Irish ship ran aground on the coast, below the castle of Deganwy, which was in English hands. The Welsh armies, which were starving, fell upon the English like animals in order to lay their hands on the food and wine that it contained. Apparently, the Welsh managed to take possession of most of the food, after which they set fire to the vessel, and we can imagine the scene as black smoke lay over the mouth of the Conwy, drifting acrid to the men on either bank. A high price to pay for the food each side so desperately needed.

After this incident, the war became increasingly bloody and violent. It is recorded that after the King's men lost a hundred soldiers one day, they came back to camp the next with the still-dripping heads of the Welsh they had killed in reprisal. The Welsh, incensed by the fact that the English callously slaughtered the men they took in battle, responded by hanging their own prisoners and throwing the bodies into the River Conwy.

To add to the desolation of the ravaged countryside, the scene when Henry at last withdrew was awful in the extreme. Piles of unburied bodies were left to rot along with the spoiled crops that Henry had ruined to stop the Welsh from obtaining supplies. His efforts had been made even more effective by activities of the Irish in Anglesey, and famine walked the land that year of 1245. The country groaned beneath the brutal hand of famine as well as war. But Henry had achieved no victory, and would have returned the following year to finish the task he had started — except that the following year, Dafydd died.

The new prince of Gwynedd was Llywelyn ab Iorwerth's grandson, the son of the prince who had fallen to his death trying to escape from the Tower. His name was Llywelyn ap Gruffudd, and it was he who picked up, as it were, the ideal of Gwynedd as overlord of the rest of Wales, where his grandfather had been forced to leave off. Within ten years, he had all but brought the whole of Wales once again beneath his overlordship, and he fought to give this ideal legal backing and some sort of validity, but his death was to mark the last flickerings of the great illusion, the dream of a native Prince of Wales who would represent the nation.

It is noticeable that battles were not always fought on the battlefield by this time in history. In the accounts of activities between the Welsh princes and the various English and other monarchs, we come across the fact that the church might often intervene, by excommunicating the prince, for instance, as happened with Prince Dafydd, son of Llywelyn the Great. Or the church might pronounce judgement in cases of dispute.

Battles were no longer as simple as they had once appeared to the very early princes. It was not enough to win land by force of arms — or even to consolidate alliances by means of dynastic marriages. Now, as Llywelyn saw only too clearly, it was necessary for the Welsh prince to have a voice in the newly developing English system of government and to protect his victories with legal machinery.

The battles of Llywelyn were mainly fought against his adversary Edward, son of Henry III. In the age of a great native Prince of Wales, there rose to confront him an equally great Prince of England.

On his accession, Llywelyn had first to establish himself and consolidate his position in Gwynedd. The kingdom was divided equally between himself and his brother Owain — and an alert Henry III was waiting nearby with an army to demand homage from the new 'lords' of Gwynedd. In addition to doing homage, Llywelyn and his brother had to agree to do military service for their 'king'. And what was to be even more significant was that Henry had previously acquired the part of Gwynedd known as the Four Cantref, which he had granted to his son, Prince Edward, in 1254.

It would not have been easy for Llywelyn to have established himself in Gwynedd when the lands had been split between himself and his brother, and eventually Owain and another brother, Dafydd, rebelled against him. Llywelyn defeated the rebels at the Battle of Bryn Derwin, on the borders of Arfon and Eifionydd, and he was then able to build on the treaties and alliances he had made with the princes of Powys and Deheubarth, as well as make himself supreme in his kingdom. His own house was in order, and Gwynedd was recovering from the bad years of war and famine. It was time to look around him.

The deputy acting for Prince Edward of England in the Four Cantref, was another of the evil villains of the period called Geoffrey de Langley. He had caused trouble in all parts of Britain, including the English court and the court of Scotland, and he continued to live up to his reputation in Wales. His activities were characterised by allowing his brutal soldiers to use violence and aggression even in sacred buildings, exacting money from the innocent by means of extortion, and generally causing great distress and misery through injustice, intimidation and fear.

By 1256, the whole of the Four Cantref was at the point of revolt, and the people begged Llywelyn to free them. He had to face the same dilemma that had confronted Owain Gwynedd and Llywelyn the Great — he had to choose between war or diplomacy. Llywelyn's course was set for the great dream, the great ideal we have already seen, that of an over-lordship of the whole of Wales, with himself as the 'Prince of Wales' doing homage to the King of England as the representative of his country.

To free the Four Cantref would be equivalent to declaring war on Henry and Prince Edward — but to allow the situation to continue and his people to carry on suffering was unthinkable. Further aggressive actions by Prince Edward and the awareness that Henry was so preoccupied with his troublesome barons that he could spare no time for Wales, brought down the balance of the scales on the side of war. Llywelyn advanced into the Four Cantref and within a week had occupied the whole territory except for one or two castles.

Like a heath-fire before the wind, Wales rose to its prince, and Llywelyn's forces marched into Meirionnydd, Ceredigion, Ystrad Tywi, Gwerthrynion and the south, restoring lands that had been taken from the Welsh and reinstating Welsh princes. Everywhere, even in the south, Llywelyn was hailed as the representative of freedom. His name on people's lips became synonymous with the ideal of a united Wales.

At last Henry III, prompted by rebel Welsh princes who had been driven from Wales by Llywelyn, took action. A royal force under Stephen Bacon advanced from Carmarthen, and tried to capture Dinefwr, but Llywelyn's troops appeared in time to relieve the siege. The king's forces, together with those of Rhys Fychan (*Rhys the Little*), the rebel prince who had been driven from Dinefwr in Llywelyn's earlier sorties in the south, were overwhelmingly defeated.

It must have seemed as though Llywelyn's star could climb no higher. Every battle he fought, every peacemaking mission he undertook, brought him even more success and the backing of the rest of Wales. He had everyone's confidence, he had ability, he had a personal charm that could win men to his side, or to see his point of view. He was perhaps one of the most charismatic personalities in the whole history of Wales.

But one man who never saw this personal charm, and whose hatred of Llywelyn was becoming increasingly bitter, was Edward, Prince of England. He had watched in helpless frustration from the walls of Chester as Llywelyn's armies occupied his Four Cantref, and he had neither the experience nor the money to cope with raising an army that could match the force of the Welsh prince.

At last, in 1257, Henry moved again and though Llywelyn tried to offer terms, he and his nobles expressing their willingness to return to the previously established situation — but without Edward being given command of the Four Cantref — Henry refused to listen, and once again invaded North Wales from Chester along the coast.

His men caused a good deal of destruction and ravaged this much-ravaged land once more, and he relieved the castle of Deganwy, but he had to retreat with Llywelyn's forces at his heels, in ignominy, and he and Llywelyn made a truce.

Henry had his hands full with the increasing rebellionsness of his barons, and even the popular feeling in England did not see Wales as a threat — it was the king himself who was regarded as the danger. And Llywelyn was now at the height of his power. In March 1258, he held a meeting with other Welsh princes, who all — except for one, Gruffudd ap Gwenwynwyn — swore him fealty. After this meeting, he made an addition to the titles his grandfather had used: 'Prince of North Wales' and 'Prince of Aberffraw and Snowdon'. From this moment on, Llywelyn ap Gruffudd was to be the first Welsh-born prince ever to use the title of 'Prince of Wales'. And he was also to be the last until Glyndŵr's rebellion in 1400.

Chapter Nine

THE BATTLES OF EDWARD I

In 1272, on the death of his father, Llywelyn's great rival and adversary Prince Edward of England, succeeded to the throne. This was to mark a new bitterness and suspicion in relations between the two countries. Whereas Llywelyn had been prepared to treat with Henry III, he did not trust Edward. Indeed, it seemed as though the world was not large enough for both Llywelyn of Wales and Edward of England to live peaceably side by side.

Llywelyn had been busy consolidating his already supreme position in Wales, capturing stubborn strongholds of the marcher barons and administering justice to rebel Welsh nobles. He had made alliances, including one with Scotland, and supported the cause of the English barons, who were then on the point of rebelling against King Henry.

But though theoretically, Wales was now united beneath the overlordship of Gwynedd and all the princes had sworn fealty to Llywelyn, it was too much to expect that such an idealistic situation would continue. Hardly had the oaths of fealty been sworn than the most powerful lord, Maredudd ap Rhys, betrayed his fellow Welsh princes and began scheming with Henry. Llywelyn was constantly aware that his supreme power had to be protected, especially against his hated enemy Prince Edward, who, more than his father, felt a personal grudge against the Welsh prince.

The leader of the English barons was Simon de Montford, with whom Llywelyn — possibly in sympathy as an 'upstart noble' against the crown — was on good terms. Hundreds of Welsh archers were with de Montford's forces against the king at the Battle of Evesham, and they were mown down pitilessly as de Montford's defeated army tried to escape.

This battle restored Henry to power in England after the various vicissitudes of the civil war known as the Baron's War, but events continued to progress like the moves on a chessboard. At one moment the king or Prince Edward was supreme, at another it was Simon de Montford. In Wales, English armies came and went, castles were seized by rebels, and then retrieved. This was a period when the Welsh people lived with constant fighting. And then, in 1272, King Henry of England died.

By the Treaty of Montgomery in 1267, Llywelyn had achieved his aim and Henry had recognised his title of Prince of Wales not only as a personal one, but also for his heirs and successors. His overlordship of all the other Welsh rulers except one, was also acknowledged. The Four Cantref were restored to Gwynedd — and among the other terms, Llywelyn undertook to pay tribute of 25,000 marks, and to provide for his brother Dafydd, who had fought against him, but with whom he had been reconciled.

Theoretically, this meant that Wales was a united nation with an overlord whose position was secure, and whose heirs would continue after him if he died. But in fact, not all the smaller princes and lords had agreed to the idea, and they were hungry for their previous independence — as always, the princes of the Welsh kingdoms fought between themselves, and if they thought it necessary, against the superiority of Gwynedd.

Early in 1274, Llywelyn discovered a plot against his life. His brother Dafydd and another powerful lord, Gruffudd ap Gwenwynwyn of Powys, were involved, but once Llywelyn moved to take action, the plotters fled to King Edward in England, where they were granted asylum.

Relations between Edward and Llywelyn were becoming increasingly strained. Llywelyn had already been summoned several times to do homage, but for one reason or another — probably genuine — he had not done so. After the plotters fled, he was summoned again, but answered that he feared for his safety since those who had conspired to murder him were being welcomed by English hands.

He had an even more urgent grievance against Edward by now since, by a previous agreement with Simon de Montford, he had contracted to marry de Montford's daughter, Eleanor. The girl had been on her way from France to her prospective bridegroom when she was captured at sea and handed over to Edward. The king offered to relinquish both Llywelyn's bride and the rebel Welsh lords if Llywelyn would do him the homage he rightfully owed.

But Llywelyn refused to treat while known enemies who had tried to kill him were being granted asylum at the English court, and while his bride was wrongfully being held a prisoner. In spite of attempts to negotiate, the situation between these proud men remained stalemate, and on 12 November, 1276, war was declared.

The name of Edward I must have been one which spelled fear to every Welshman. His assaults on Wales — apart from attempts when he was very young to hold the Four Cantref, which were marked by inexperience — were models of organisation and planning. Edward's armies were like machines, they were huge, efficient and relentless. This campaign was to cost him £23,000 and it lasted for a year.

Four armed divisions marched upon Wales to occupy the main sections of Welsh-held territory, and Edward himself led a force west from Chester. An English fleet landed in Anglesey to seize and destroy Llywelyn's harvests on the island which was Gwynedd's 'granary'. Most of the lesser Welsh princes, seeing the hopelessness of the situation, made their own peace with Edward, and the united princedom of Wales disintegrated before Llywelyn's eyes.

Edward put into operation the tactics which were to mark his further successful conquests in Wales later. As he advanced he ordered work to be begun on castles in strategic positions, to control the area he had conquered. Densely wooded land of the sort that the Welsh had traditionally used as their bases for guerilla attacks on invaders or enemies, were cut down. Roads were cleared.

On 10 November, 1277, Llywelyn made peace with Edward at the signing of the Treaty of Rhuddlan. In this humiliating treaty, he lost most of the lands he had added to his own over the previous thirty years, as well as the homage of most of the other Welsh princes, and his claims to former conquests. He had to undertake to pay huge sums in tribute to Edward. What he did retain was his title of Prince of Wales, but the position from which he ruled was very much reduced from his former position of supremacy.

Relations did improve after this between Llywelyn and Edward, however. Llywelyn swore his allegiance to Edward, who not only gave Eleanor de Montford away at her wedding to Llywelyn in Worcester Cathedral, but also footed the bill for the celebrations. But this more settled state of affairs was not to last. Within five years, the scene would change dramatically.

Disagreements, particularly over that thorny Welsh topic, boundaries, arose thick and fast, and since it was often unclear by the terms of the treaty, which areas the relevant lands belonged in — Welsh or border — it was also not clear whether they should be settled by Welsh law or Marcher law. Grievances and complaints — even from Llywelyn's brother Dafydd, who had fought for Edward against his brother and had been presented with the castle of Denbigh as a reward — began to mount against the English administrators and officials for the crown.

Grievances simmered over a period of time, and the country seemed on the surface to be at peace. But when the flare-up came, it was not just a few isolated local incidents. The whole of Wales became involved, and in 1282, unable to stomach any more interference in its affairs and the affairs of its people by English and crown officialdom, Wales howled for war.

On the night before Palm Sunday, Llywelyn's brother Dafydd mounted an attack on Hawarden Castle, and followed this up with successful attacks on Ruthin, Hope and Dinas Brân, though Flint Castle and Rhuddlan Castle succeeded in holding out against the Welsh forces. A council of Welsh lords declared war at Denbigh, and the rebellion spread through the whole of the country.

Edward's campaign was this time to cost him over £60,000, but he was determined to bring Llywelyn and the troublesome Welsh down for good and all. He employed the same tactics which had been so successful previously, and sent in three separate armies from Chester, Montgomery and Carmarthen. Once he had the south under his control, he was able to turn to the more tricky problem of the north, and not only led the main forces himself from a base at Rhuddlan, but planned ambitious tactics to bring Snowdonia, that outpost which had so many times kept the freedom of the Welsh alive in the past, to heel.

Edward sent another army to Anglesey, and its commander, Luke de Tany, had orders to construct a bridge of boats across the Menai Straits so that his forces could gain access to the mainland. This way, Edward's armies would be able to attack Snowdonia from two sides. But de Tany was warned not to cross to the mainland until the main army under Edward's own command had reached Conwy.

The ambitious commander took no heed of his orders, however, and in spite of a temporary truce between Llywelyn and Edward while the Archbishop of Canterbury made attempts to negotiate terms for peace, he led his forces across the new bridge to the mainland on 6 November 1282. They met a resounding defeat at the hands of the Welsh, who intercepted them at Moel y Don, and there was a great loss of life as they were driven back to escape as best they could. Many of the soldiers were drowned in the rising tide, and several high-ranking English nobles were killed. Luke de Tany's ambitions came to nothing, since he too died in the battle.

Llywelyn went south, and in December, was engaged in trying to keep the English away from the strategic stronghold of Builth Castle. His army was defending Orewin Bridge across the Irfon, and in this relatively minor engagement, a humble man-at-arms or esquire, Adam de Frankton, encountered Llywelyn on his own, apart from the main body of the fighting forces. Seeing only an unknown Welsh horseman, Adam de Frankton attacked Llywelyn and ran him through with his lance, in ignorance of his identity.

The facts surrounding the death of this last Welsh 'Prince of Wales' are dramatically uncertain. It is not clear exactly what Llywelyn was doing separated from the main body of his troops when he was killed, though there are hints that Llywelyn was being betrayed by his own nobles. Certainly there were many who would have been only too happy to see him fall into an ambush, and a mysterious letter that was apparently discovered on his body might have shed some light on the situation, but its contents were never revealed.

There are tales that Llywelyn went off to raise the garrison at Builth Castle to his cause, riding a horse whose shoes had been reversed in order to confuse pursuers. He is reported to have asked for a priest when he was dying, even though he had been excommunicated. What is certain is that his head was cut off to be sent to Edward. It was eventually taken to London to be displayed, in the manner customary for traitors, on Tower Bridge.

His body was buried at the Cistercian Abbey of Cwmhir, and a monument on the roadside at Cilmeri records that: 'Near this spot was killed our Prince Llywelyn 1282.'

With Llywelyn's death, the heart of Wales collapsed. Llywelyn's brother Dafydd, who had turned-coat so many times that it was a wonder anyone ever trusted anything he said, declared himself the new Prince of Wales, and tried to fight on, but within only a few months he was in Edward's hands, having been handed over to the English forces, so we are told, by 'men of his own tongue'. He met a terrible traitor's death at Shrewsbury in October, 1283, when he was dragged through the streets to be hanged, drawn and mercifully beheaded before his body was quartered. His head was placed with Llywelyn's on Tower Bridge, and Edward I was the conqueror of Wales. He was to give the country a new system of shires that altered the face of the ancient kingdoms and princedoms — and he was to give Wales its first English Prince of Wales.

Lament for Llywelyn ap Gruffudd

Heart cold in the breast with terror, grieving
For a king, oak door, of Aberffraw.
Bright gold was bestowed by his hand,
A gold chaplet befitted him.
A gold king's gold cups come not to me, mirth
Of Llywelyn; not for me free raiment.
I grieve for a prince, hawk free of reproach,
I grieve for the ill that befell him,
I grieve for the loss, I grieve for the lot,
I grieve to hear how he was wounded . . .
Mine, rage at the Saxon who robbed me,
Mine, before death, the need to lament,
Mine, with good reason, to rave against God
Who has left me without him,
Mine to praise him, unstinting, unstilled,
Mine to be ever mindful of him,
Mine all my lifetime sorrowing for him,
Since mine is the woe, mine the weeping . . .
See you not the rush of wind and rain?
See you not the oaks lash each other?
See you not the ocean scourging the shore?
See you not the truth is portending?
See you not the sun hurtling the sky?
See you not that the stars have fallen?
Have you no belief in God, foolish men?
See you not that the world is ending?
Ah God, that the sea would cover the land!
What is left us that we should linger?
No place to flee from terror's prison,
No place to live; wretched is living!
No counsel, no clasp, no path left open
One way to be freed from fear's sad strife . . .
All the weak, all the strong he kept safe:
All children now cry in their cradles.
Little good it did me to dupe me,
Leaving me a head, with him headless.
Head that slain made fear unhateful,
Head that slain made surrender best,
Head of a soldier, head of praise,
Head of a duke, a dragon's head,
Head of fair Llywelyn, sharp the world's fear,
An iron spike through it,
Head of my lord, harsh pain is mine,
Head of my spirit left speechless,
Head that had honour in nine-hundred lands,
Nine-hundred feasts for him,
Head of a king, his hand hurled iron,

Head of a proud hawk, he forced a breach,
Head of a kingly wolf thrust foremost,
Head of kings, heaven be his haven!

Gruffudd ab yr Ynad Coch

Chapter Ten

WELSH MERCENARIES AND BOWMEN

Military strategy and tactics had changed enormously since the Dark Ages, where most battles were primitive affairs fought at river crossings, since that was where the enemy would be at his most vulnerable. But there had always been adventurers who took eagerly to the trade of mercenary and became professional soldiers whose services were for hire, usually to the highest bidder.

The Welsh had long since been famed for their skill as fighters, and the old tribal laws had even laid down a sort of 'conscription' where for six weeks in each year, the men of every tribe went out on a marauding exercise. In the everyday living of the principality, provision was made for a fighting force which could be assembled at a moment's notice. Every young man, if summoned by his prince or lord, would take up arms immediately.

As we have already seen, the Welsh were skilled at guerilla warfare and commando-type raids and forays rather than as a precision unit. They had always armed themselves lightly and carried all their equipment with them. No trains of baggage or clumsy catapults or towers on make-shift platforms for these men who could scale the heights of the Snowdonia mountains and cross river estuaries with just their bare hands and their skill with the sturdy hill ponies they rode.

Ambushes were the favourite tactic of Welsh warriors and they would follow up an initial hail of arrows with a fierce charge that allowed them to hack at their enemies with sword and spear before they made a quick retreat, usually leaving the foe bewildered and bloody. Since the Welsh were able to move so quickly in their own terrain, they could just fade into the mists, and few invading armies dared to try and follow them.

In the twelfth century, Giraldus Cambrensis (Gerald the Welshman) described the Welsh as:

> 'entirely bred up to the use of arms; for not only the nobles but all the people are trained to war, and when the trumpet sounds the alarm the husbandman rushes as eagerly from his plough as the courtier from his court.'

In his vivid word-pictures, Giraldus tells us that 'they anxiously study the defence of their country and their liberty; for these they fight, for these they undergo hardships; and for these willingly sacrifice their lives; they esteem it a disgrace to die in bed, an honour to die in the field of battle.'

He gives us, too, a first-hand description of what the Welsh warriors wore to go to battle, and what they carried: 'light arms which do not impede their agility, small coats of mail, bundles of arrows and long lances, helmets and shields.' Occasionally they wore leg greaves with iron plates.

'The higher class go to battle mounted on swift and generous steeds, which their country produces,' he further informs us, 'but the greater part of the people fight on foot on account of the marshy nature and unevenness of the soil. The horsemen, as their situation or occasion requires, willingly serve as infantry, in attacking or retreating and they either walk barefooted, or make use of high shoes, roughly constructed with untanned leather. In time of peace the young men, by penetrating the deep recesses of the woods and climbing the tops of mountains, learn by practice to endure fatigue through day and night; and as they meditate on war during peace they acquire the art of fighting by accustoming themselves to the use of the lance and by inuring themselves to hard exercise.'

Giraldus also gives a colourful account of what the Welsh must have looked like when an enemy confronted them in battle. These are very much the guerilla tactics that we have already noted:

'— this nation is very severe in the first attack, terrible by their clamour and looks, filling the air with horrid shouts and the deep-toned clangour of very long trumpets, swift and rapid in their advances and frequent throwing of darts . . . Their mode of fighting consists in chasing the enemy or retreating. This light-armed people, relying more on their activity than their strength, cannot struggle for the field of battle, enter into close engagement, or endure long and severe actions.'

However, Giraldus goes on to add:

'Though defeated and put to flight on one day they are ready to resume the combat on the next, neither dejected by their loss nor by their dishonour and although perhaps they do not display great fortitude in open engagements and regular conflicts, yet they harass the enemy by ambuscades and nightly sallies. Hence neither oppressed by hunger or cold, nor fatigued by martial labours, nor despondent in adversity, but ready after defeat to return immediately to action and again endure the dangers of war they are as easy to overcome in a single battle as difficult to subdue in a protracted war.'

Right from the early period when their nation was in the process of being forged from the jumbled masses of conquered, conquerors, invaders and other tribes which inhabited the area which was later to be called Wales, the Welsh lacked the strength of arms which first the Romans and later the various English kingdoms tried to use to subdue them. But they drew on their own strengths. These were their boundless native energy, their resilience and their ability to adapt seeming weakness to their advantage.

An example of this ingenuity is in the development of their greatest weapon, the longbow, dsecribed by Giraldus Cambrensis as 'made neither of horn, ash or yew but of wild elm; ugly, unpolished and uncouth but amazingly stiff, large and strong, equally suited to long or short shooting'. People who had experience of fighting the Welsh might have added that this description could just as well have been of the warriors of Wales themselves.

Shorter bows, notably the crossbow, were already in use in the armies of twelfth century powers and were capable of inflicting heavy damage on the opposing forces. But the arrows of the longbow could be fired faster than those of a crossbow, which was never able to shoot more than three bolts per minute. The longbow, in skilled hands, could shoot up to twelve shots in the course of a minute, and when ranks of archers were shooting simultaneously, the effect was a terrifying thick hail of arrows, which was as deadly as machine-gun fire.

In fact, it could well have been more deadly, since it was certainly more accurate than a machine-gun. An archer of the Middle Ages would have considered himself a disgrace to his profession if at a range of two hundred and fifty yards, even one of his twelve-a-minute shots missed.

The accuracy of the archers of the Middle Ages was something that was marvelled at by friend and foe alike, and was recorded with bated breath by chroniclers. It was claimed that at one battle, a Genoan crossbowman in the enemy ranks shook his fist over the top of his protective shield at the English, a hundred paces away. Immediately, twenty archers (who might very well have been from Wales) loosed arrows towards him. Later, when he was taken, his arm was bristling with arrows. Eighteen of the twenty shafts had found their mark in his forearm. And this was only one of many such instances which recorded almost unbelievable feats of archery.

All that has ever been written, sung and said about those legendary men of earlier days with their longbows on their shoulders, and their phenomenally powerful arms and shoulders, is happily difficult to contradict. They were the real heroes of the great battles of the Middle Ages, and it is gratifying to note that, whatever the army, the bowmen whose amazing feats of arms quite often turned the tide of battle, could very well have been Welshmen. For although the men of Cheshire and various other areas were to gain almost legendary fame for their prowess with the bow, it was the Welsh who were the first and the best longbowmen in the world at that time.

In 1182, at the siege of Abergavenny, a door made of four-inch thick solid oak was pierced right through by Welsh arrows. The sight of the arrows with their iron tips visible on the inside of the door was thought to be such a wonder that they were displayed to passers-by for many years afterwards, just as they had found their marks from the bows of the Welsh archers.

The power of the longbow was demonstrably phenomenal. It is recorded that one of the knights of the Marcher baron William de Braose was skewered by an arrow which went through his armour, piercing the skirt of his hauberk and his mail hose or breeches, into his thigh, through his saddle (which was leather and wood) into his horse's flank, killing the horse. Another rider, similarly armed, was pinned to his saddle by an arrow through his hip (and through the casing protecting his hip). When he turned his horse round, another arrow pinned him in exactly the same manner on the other side. How he eventually managed to dismount from his horse has not, unfortunately, been recorded!

It is sometimes claimed that the Welsh invented the longbow, but what is more accurate is to say that when it evolved from the bows-and-arrows which had been in use since the dawn of time, it was the Welsh — particularly the warriors of South Wales, Gwent and Morgannwg — who were the first to develop the power of the longbow for their own use and gain the skills which were to give them mastery of the weapon.

Traditionally, the Welsh used the lance for throwing, and had never favoured the crossbow, even though it was considered the most deadly weapon of those times. But there were great advantages in the longbow, mainly, so far as the Welsh were concerned, its lack of complicated mechanism for loading and shooting, and the fact that it could hold its own even against heavily armed opposition. The bow was in fact the only weapon which could offer a serious threat to an armoured and mounted knight in the hands of a man on foot who might only be lightly armed.

The Welsh increased the size and thickness of their bows in order to compensate for the great distances and rocky terrain where they were obliged to do their hunting and their fighting, and it was by trial and error that they discovered what size to make their weapons in order for them to be utterly reliable.

Even the English kings came to fear Welsh bowmen, with good reason for their skills were spectacular, and efforts were even made to try and stop the Welsh from travelling if they were armed with bows. But since they could not beat the bowmen, the English kings took the wisest alternative and encouraged the bowmen to join them — or join their armies, at any rate.

Even as early as the reign of Henry I of England, bowmen had played a dramatic part in the victories of the English armies, but it was probably Edward I, who came to know at first hand exactly how devastating the archers of Wales could be, who set the formal precedent of employing troops of Welsh bowmen in the service of the English crown. Good archers were valuable assets and since a bowman had to keep in constant practice, it was considered more important for the yeomen and able-bodied potential fighting men of England to spend their holiday days at the butts, practising archery instead of indulging in idle pastimes — like golf and football for instance. Both of these were at various times banned so that the men of England would not be distracted from the serious business of archery.

The Welsh had always rallied round their princes and their own leaders. After the death of Llywelyn, there was no national leader to command them, no-one to make use of the fighting skills they had cultivated. There are records of Welsh bowmen joining the armies of rulers outside Wales, and strange though it may seem, a contingent of Welsh bowmen would henceforth form an important part of the armies of the Kings of England. Although Wales herself still would not yield her independence to the England crown, it was the Welsh bowmen who were to swing the balance of war in favour of the England at such historic battles as Crecy and Agincourt.

Though not a part of England, there were areas of Wales which were becoming integrated, and when Edward I conducted his campaigns against the Welsh, there were bowmen from Gwent and Crickhowell in his army, as well as a hundred picked archers from Macclesfield who were paid an extremely high wage since they were considered so important a part of his force. His son, Edward of Caernarvon was appointed the first English Prince of Wales, and there were loyal bands of Welsh bowmen — and foot soldiers as well — who formed a part of the army that went north with him to Scotland.

Welsh archers had already served the crown in Scotland in the Scottish Wars. After Edward I had brought Wales to heel, he made war on the Scots. We have seen that some of the Welsh fighting force had left Llywelyn's army to join the English, and it comes as no surprise to hear that there were over 10,000 Welsh bowmen in the armies that marched up to Scotland in 1298 under Edward. When the English attacked the Scottish troops which had prepared for battle at Falkirk, it was the deadly accuracy of thousands of Welsh arrows which gave victory to Edward, at the cost of the lives of ten thousand Scottish soldiers.

Welsh bowmen fought in the English armies against the Scottish leaders William Wallace and Robert Bruce. At Bannockburn, there were five hundred men from Glamorgan in the English army, and even in the terrible debacle of the rout that occurred, it was the bowmen who might possibly have saved the day, if the Scottish attacks had not been so savage.

Wales was represented at the great battles of Crecy, Poitiers and Agincourt. Welsh archers were needed and they did not fail. But though they were highly valued for their skill with the longbow, it was recorded that the army commanders found them difficult to deal with. They were, so we are told, invariably quarrelsome and inclined to start brawling with comrades-in-arms of other nationalities, including the English. The Welsh would probably have put matters differently, and had their own version of events. They were just defending their Welsh identity, they would have claimed, protecting their right to be different. Wherever they went, it seemed, the Welsh continued to assert their independence and to fight for their colourful individuality.

The Exile of Cambria

(Which might have been the words felt by the Welsh bowmen)

O Wales! as I leave you, the light fades away,
And faint and more faint beams the bright orb of day;
The winds are all hush'd and the ocean serene,
Aye! calm as the lakes thy blue Valleys between.
Oh this is the hour when darkness is near
When memory mixes my smile and my tear,
My service by a foreign king is in demand
And the whole world is drowing in the longing for my land.

Traditional Welsh Song

Chapter Eleven

THE BATTLES OF OWAIN GLYNDŴR

There are almost as many legends about Owain Glyndŵr as there are about Arthur, and it is significant that both these great heroes have unknown graves. Nobody ever knew where they were buried, and the inference is that they did not actually die, but are lingering somewhere — in the mountains, tradition has it — so that if they are needed, they can return to fight on.

In fact, Owain Glyndŵr is possibly the most dramatic of the great national heroes of Wales. He was not born a prince, but he was the last Welshman to lead an uprising of any magnitude against the English. There had been other rebellions before that of Glyndŵr. Wales had grown accustomed to the overlordship of the kings of England and the English officers and civil servants who now administered crown lands and the new systems of government which had been imposed by Edward I along with his new castles and shire towns, but the country as a whole had never really accepted them. The towns in particular had become anglicized and hateful to the people of Wales. Always, in some corner of the country, some small rebellion seethed against one of the many injustices which were perpetuated against the Welsh.

Under Owain, the old ideal of Welsh independence, the revival of the aim of a united Wales under its own ruler, the last attempt to rid Wales of foreign interference, were what the country was fighting for. In this last great rebellion of note, these Welsh dreams flared, flickered magnificently, and died for the last time.

Though he was not born expecting to be the leader of his country — even, rather unwilling to take on this role — Owain Glyndŵr was to be the last Welshman to hold the title of Prince in Wales. But as with many romantic figures, the way he is popularly imagined — a dashing young man with blazing eyes and a sword glittering in his hand — is not really accurate.

Owain Glyndŵr was no romantic and blazing-eyed young leader. In 1399, when the rebellion was on the point of breaking out, he was a middle-aged country gentleman of great respectability. He had led a full life, and was quite content to live in peaceful retirement after a distinguished military career, his sons and daughters grown up with families of their own.

Even though he was descended by blood both from the royal line of Llywelyn the Last and from the princes of South Wales, Owain had accepted — as did most of the Welsh gentry and nobility — the status quo and the overlordship of the then king of England, Richard II, son of the Black Prince, both of whom had large and loyal bodies of Welsh supporters.

Welsh loyalty to the English crown, and in particular to the young English princes who had over the years been created 'Prince of Wales' since the death of Llywelyn, roused the Welsh to indignation at the betrayal of Richard II into the hands of the usurper Henry Bolingbroke — later to become Henry IV — at Flint Castle. When this was followed by Henry's seizure of the throne, and Richard was mysteriously imprisoned at Pontefract and never heard of again, his cause and the possibility of restoring him to his kingdom played a large part in motivating the rebellion.

Shortly after Richard's betrayal, the new and extremely unpopular King Henry supported one of his cronies, Lord Grey of Ruthin, in yet another of those troublesome disputes involving boundaries and borders — this time in favour of Lord Grey's claim for a piece of land he had unlawfully appropriated. This set light to the fuse which was to fire the rebellion, for the man who was standing against Lord Grey was none other than Owain ap Gruffudd, lord of Glyndyfrdwy — otherwise known as Owain Glyndŵr.

Owain, who had spent a lifetime as a military leader fighting for the English crown, was so incensed at this flagrant piece of royal injustice — a mere example of the many such injustices the people of Wales were suffering at the hands of English officialdom — that he set out to fight not for the English crown, but for a different monarchy which would put such injustices to rights. He fought for himself, but it was vaguely rumoured that he was acting for Richard II until that monarch was able to return to his kingdom.

Owain took as his title 'Prince of Wales', which the usurper Bolingbroke had already bestowed on his son, and using his estates in north-east Wales as a base, gathered himself an army from the ranks of all who felt they were not satisfied with the state of affairs in the country. The people were whole-hearted in their support, and it was reported that many sold their cattle in order to buy horses, saddles, bows and other weapons of war.

The Welsh have always possessed the Celtic belief in signs and omens, and the heavens themselves were alive with portents in 1400 —

the year Owain's rebellion burst with the force of a dam giving way, across Wales. The stream where the head of the last native prince, Llywelyn ap Gruffudd, had been washed after being hacked from his body to be taken to Edward I, suddenly ran with blood for a whole day; and four small bells at the shrine of St Edward at Westminster rang loudly of their own volition, with superhuman power, four times during another day. All the fates seemed to be setting the seal of approval on this uprising, and indicating that Wales had once more found herself a prince in her time of need.

Owain's opening attacks were surprise raids, the first on Lord Grey's castle of Ruthin. His men entered as the gates of the town were opened at dawn, surged through setting fire to everything that would burn, and drove away all the cattle they saw. Rather surprisingly there do not seem to have been any casualties, probably because Owain, in the great tradition of Welsh fighting men, had sprung his guerilla attack so effectively that there was little resistance. Following this attack, Owain's army, which became proudly known throughout Wales as 'Owain's Children', similarly attacked other castles and towns at Denbigh, Flint, Hawarden, Holt and Rhuddlan.

They proceeded along the border from Chester to Oswestry, and then south, heading for Welshpool. When Henry IV arrived in Wales with an army, Owain and his men could not be found, and they continued to remain frustratingly invisible so that the king had no opportunity to engage them in battle.

Possibly Owain's troops were not quite the picturesque and romantic army tradition describes to us, eyes alight with national fervour and the heroic songs of their land on their lips, but they must certainly have been a sight to strike fear into the hearts of any enemies of Wales. One thing there was no mistaking was their devotion to their leader and their cause.

Welshmen had flocked to join their new Prince, not only from Wales but home from college at London or Oxford; or from other parts of England where they might have sought employment. Welsh mercenaries hurried home from France, and arrived to swell Owain's army from the hot climes of the East. They had idealistic hopes of patriotic and personal glory, and prided themselves afterwards on the fact that they had played a part in so historic a rising.

One family even went so far as to choose a new motto and change their coat of arms to reflect their participation in the revolt.

National feeling was entirely on Owain's side. It was reported that he had sworn to remove the hated English tongue — the language in which official business and government affairs had to be legally conducted — from Wales, and he and his armies were welcomed and given assistance everywhere.

On occasion, Owain had 30,000 men at his call, but sometimes — as happened at Welshpool — his troops were few and were outnumbered so that they were obliged to carry out guerilla tactics of breaking and running, withdrawing into the woods or into mountainous territory, or even going back to a seemingly innocent and peaceful life — until the next opportunity arose for them to steal away in the night to join another band of 'Owain's Children' and fall on the English where they would least expect it. The rebellion was an on-going thing, and must have turned almost into a way of living for the men who followed their guerilla leader.

Of all the national leaders of the Welsh, Owain Glyndŵr is the one who has been the most romanticised in song and story. His battles too, and his rising itself, have been painted in the mysterious colours of legend. There is a great deal we do not know about Owain's revolt, his plans, his armies. And the fact that he was so elusive — that he and his men could apparently melt away at will if an army trapped them or tried to engage them in battle — only adds authenticity to the tales which the Welsh repeated to each other in the firelit evenings.

For the first few years when his revolt was raging throughout Wales, gathering in momentum and force even as King Henry made more and more severe efforts to punish and subdue the Welsh, Owain's tactics were those of a first-class guerilla leader. His success can be seen from the fact that Henry and the other English leaders hardly ever managed to engage Owain's forces in a decisive battle — though if they had to, the Welsh were prepared to stand and fight. All the funds which Henry spent trying to subdue this rebellion, the expeditions he sent to Wales, were largely fruitless.

Owain was magnificent, and to his friends as well as his enemies, appeared to possess attributes which were super-human. Tales which would be referred to later by Shakespeare in *Henry IV*, of Owain being able to conjure spirits and storms, of his powers as a wizard, of being able to inhabit other bodies to his own, were soon being popularly repeated by those who feared, as well as those who loved, the Welsh leader.

In the summer of 1401, Owain defeated a strong army of Flemish and English soldiers at Hyddgen, a valley high up in the Pumlumon mountains. King Henry tried to pin Glyndŵr down later that year with another army, ravaging the country as he marched to Strata Florida. He did not encounter the rebel leader, but as he was taking reprisals on Cardiganshire and its people, Owain's troops suddenly made a swift and daring attack on Henry's army and inflicted heavy losses before disappearing into the mist with the tents, arms and horses of Prince Hal, Henry's son.

Furious, Henry passed prohibitive measures through Parliament to try and keep the Welsh down, but by 1402, Owain had emerged from the guise of national guerilla leader and was beginning to behave as a diplomatic leader of his people, a statesman. And the whole of Wales was unequivocally and solidly behind him.

As skilled in diplomacy as in guerilla war, Owain summoned Welsh parliaments and entered into negotiations with the lords of Ireland; he signed a treaty with France and made attempts to treat with the Scots and with English nobles who had grievances against King Henry, forming alliances against the king. He had ambitious plans for encouraging Welsh culture. And he continued to protect his country by winning victories at the Battle of the Fyrnwy — where his old adversary Lord Grey was taken prisoner, and two thousand of Henry's men fell — and the Battle of Bryn Glas.

Professor O.M. Edwards has this to say about Bryn Glas:

> 'In summer (of 1402) Rhys Gethin and a small army met the levies of the border counties at Bryn Glas. The Welsh borderers in the English ranks joined their Welsh countrymen and turned their arrows against their own army; and the English army, which had hurried on for fear that the Welshmen would not give battle, broke into disastrous flight.'

This battle also brought the English lord Edmund Mortimer, uncle of the righful heir to the English throne, into Owain's hands as a prisoner. Owain made the most of his valuable captive, and married Mortimer to his daughter. Mortimer was to become almost more Welsh than his new family, and suffered with them when they were besieged at Harlech Castle. Mortimer died in 1409 at Harlech from starvation, before the siege was lifted.

The story of the remaining battles of Owain Glyndŵr follows much the same pattern as those of the other Welsh princes who had attempted to gain independence for a united Wales. Henry of England brought a huge army which advanced on Wales from three bases, and which was driven out not by the Welsh, who wisely kept their distance, but by torrential rain-storms and heavy winds. Little wonder that the legends about Owain's powers to control the weather increased incredibly after this.

An army led by Prince Hal, later to become Henry V, fared better when it marched the length of Wales in 1402. Castles were captured and the people were subdued. It seems that there was little sense of chivalry on either side — perhaps because each was so determined not to be defeated. But whereas there had previously been some feeling of honour and responsibility towards prisoners, women and children, so that those who broke the code were treated by other lords with outrage and disgust, war was now considered to be to the death, with no mercy shown. This attitude, too, is reflected in the increasing number of atrocities which were perpetuated on prisoners after a battle.

The English continued to try and take Welsh-held castles and lands, while Owain and his armies did the same with the possessions owned by the king and his allies. By 1406, though, Owain was more or less in control of Wales, but his fortunes were waning. He had many allies, but all his plans seemed to come to nothing, and the alliances he had made were weakened by murders, deaths, loss of friends.

Nothing came of his plans. He was never defeated in any conclusive battle, but tragedies ate away at his position and his own life. His family — his wife, his daughter and four grand-children — were taken prisoner by the English in 1409 when Harlech Castle fell after being beseiged by 1000 men.

Towards the end, it seems as though Owain turned into some sort of visionary symbol of what Wales might have become if fate had chanced differently. In 1412, he was offered a free pardon, but would not accept it, and lived the remainder of his life as a fugitive. He is thought to have died in 1416, at the home of one of his daughters at Monnington in Herefordshire, but since no-one has any idea of where he was buried, even the poets who wrote at that time did not mourn for him. In the hearts of the people of Wales, he is not dead, but will live for ever, at one with the mist and the mountains, an eternal part of the Wales he loved and fought for.

Men of Harlech

(Harlech castle was the battle headquarters of Owain Glyndŵr's revolt)

Fierce the beacon light is flaming,
With its tongues of fire proclaiming,
"Chieftians, sundered to your shaming,
Strongly now unite!"
At the call all Arfon rallies,
War cries rend her hills and valleys,
Troop on troop, with headlong sallies,
Hurtle to the fight.
Chiefs lie dead and wounded,
Yet, where first 'twas grounded,
Freedom's flag still holds the crag —
Her trumpet still is sounded.
O there we'll keep her banner flying
While the pale lips of the dying
Echo to our shout defying
"Harlech for the right!"

Shall the Saxon army shake you,
Smite, pursue and overtake you?
Men of Harlech, God shall make you
Victors, blow for blow!
As the rivers of Eryri
Sweep the vale with flooded fury,
Gwalia from her mountain eyrie
Thunders on the foe!
Now, avenging Briton,
Smite as he has smitten!
Let your rage on history's page
In Saxon blood be written!
His lance is long, but yours is longer,
Strong his sword, but yours is stronger!
One stroke more! and then your wronger
At your feet lies low!

Chapter Twelve

A KING FROM WALES

In the best tradition of heroic princes from 'beyond the sea' like Bonnie Prince Charlie, Wales had her own son who made a triumphant return from exile to sweep everything before him and possess himself not only of Wales, but of the crown of England. Henry Tudor, who was to become Henry VII of England at the Battle of Bosworth Field in 1485, was descended from the Tudors of Penmynydd in Anglesey, and through them, from the Welsh princes. But he was also descended through his mother from John of Gaunt and the blood royal of England ran in his veins. For the first time in the history of England and Wales, the crown of England rested on the brow of a Welshman.

The revolt of Owain Glyndŵr had been a desperate and violent attempt to reaffirm the Welsh identity and rally the people to an awareness of just how their nation was being trampled beneath the heel of English injustice and reduced almost to submission. But even though the revolt had apparently failed, Wales was more nationally aware than she had ever been, and there was a new anticipation and alertness in the minds of many Welsh people. The old legends and tales which the bards had once sung by the firesides of their princes sprang into being again.

Stories of Arthur and of his eventual return if his country should need him — and more recent pledges that Glyndŵr himself would also return — were told with new zeal. The people of Wales waited for their champion to make his appearance — and in the meantime, being as we have seen, a nation whose high courage and valour made them at home on the field of battle, they took up arms for both the houses of York and Lancaster during the Wars of the Roses.

After the revolt of Glyndŵr, the Welsh appeared to be in a worse situation than ever. New laws were passed forbidding Welshmen to acquire land within the limits of border towns. They were not allowed to hold municipal offices, carry arms, fortify their houses. They were banned from holding responsible positions in the service of the English, and were generally placed so that they were not exactly treated as outlaws, but were certainly regarded as legally suspect and untrustworthy. In the same way as possible trouble-makers have always been treated, they were forbidden to hold assemblies or gather together without having been granted special permission.

All of this was humiliating and frustrating to the majority of honest Welshmen. It was beyond insult that they should be put in the position of serfs in their own territory. But England feared — as it had always done — more national uprising, and there might have been a genuine danger of this. There were many real outlaws, men who had fought for Glyndŵr, and who were joined as the years wore on by soldiers returning from war, and other mercenaries whose livelihood was war, pillage, looting and fighting.

A rather romantic picture is sometimes painted of the Welsh outlaw's life, as it was recorded in the poetry of some of the men who lived it. Great fun, a sort of idyllic version of a Celtic Robin Hood, whiling away the idle hours beneath the greenwood trees.

In fact, though, these outlaw bands were indeed still fighting for the cause of their country, both physically and in the verses of their poems. Wales, under the new legislation, was being reduced to a nation of slaves. Even the gentry were having to beg for the necessities of making their living — a plough or an ox. As for the ordinary people, still recovering from the crippling blows dealt on the countryside by the Black Death, life was just a bitter struggle to survive. And to add to their miseries, the whole country was to be plunged into the fluctuating fortunes of the Wars of the Roses.

In spite of the fact that there were few actual battles of note on Welsh soil in these conflicts between York and Lancaster, the Welsh were heavily involved on both sides. The eastern side of Wales was strongly Yorkist, largely because of support for the Mortimer family which possessed enormous estates in the Marches. But in the south, there was powerful support for the Lancastrian Sir William Herbert of Raglan.

When Sir William (who became Earl of Pembroke just before his death) was defeated at the Battle of Banbury in 1469, the whole of Wales must have gone into mourning. Two thousand Welshmen, noble and lesser born, perished with him, either on the battlefield or else, as he did, by the executioner's axe afterwards. And just as the bards of old had lamented the passing of the warriors of Gododdin at Catterick, their successors of the Middle Ages celebrated the deaths of these Welsh fighting men who had given their lives for the sake of a quarrel between the English nobility, in which Wales was not really involved.

At first, popular feeling in Wales was inclined to back the Yorkists, for the claimant had some Welsh threads in his lineage and was able to trace his descent from Llywelyn ap Gruffudd's daughter, Gwladys. But as the struggle progressed, when it was made known that the young Henry Tudor, who as well as being descended from the royal line of England, could also trace his descent from the royal line of Wales, planned to claim the English throne, the whole of Wales began to simmer like a huge cauldron.

The advent of Henry Tudor, and the eventual rise of the Tudors to power on the throne of England, was to Wales like the coming true of a fairy tale. Henry was to be their gallant champion and knight, he would ride from the mists of his exile and deliver his country and his people from the bonds of Saxon oppression. The bards and seers had been foretelling the coming of a great deliverer for a long time, and now that they could see his face, as it were, they let Arthur and Glyndŵr fade into the background while they focussed all their hopes on the young Tudor lad who had been born in Pembroke Castle, but was now in exile in Brittany.

Typical of the excitement and romance that clings even today round the stories of the coming of Henry Tudor into his own, is the tradition of 'The King's Window' at Mostyn Hall, near Holywell. It is claimed that Henry came secretly to Mostyn before the Battle of Bosworth, to discuss plans with his loyal supporters. He was betrayed and when a troop of men arrived at the Hall to capture him, he only just managed to escape through a narrow aperture that was pointed out ever afterwards as 'The King's Window'.

Since it is recorded that Richard ap Howel of Mostyn was one of Henry's followers who later brought droves of cattle to feed the army, to a rendezvous at the Long Mountain where Henry's supporters were secretly gathering in 1485, just before Bosworth, this could, like other such tales, well be true.

There is no story which contains all the romance of a lost prince, an exile, a gathering of loyal support and a happy ending from the point of view of the Welsh, which can beat the story of Henry Tudor as a wonderful example of the sudden shining of Wales' national awareness and pride after years of dark misery and degradation. Henry's grand-daughter Elizabeth Tudor was immensely proud of her Welsh lineage, and one of her favourite ladies, who was in her service from her childhood, was the Welsh-speaking Blanche Parry. Elizabeth claimed to be able to speak the Welsh language herself.

As for Henry VII, whatever his faults as a man and a ruler of

England, he made it clear right from the start that it was as a Welshman that he had come to fight for the crown. As he rode to Bosworth the standard that fluttered above his head was a red dragon on a field of white and green sarsenet — the standard of the almost legendary Cadwaladr, one of the seventh century princes of Wales, which had also been the standard of Rhodri the Great.

The main task of Wales during the Wars of the Roses, was to provide armies for York and for Lancaster. At the Battle of Mortimer's Cross on February 2, 1461, the Welsh Yorkists faced the Welsh Lancastrians and the day went to Edward of York. Owen Tudor — he who had married Henry V's widow, Katharine of France, and who was the grandfather of the young Henry currently in exile — had roused his elderly bones to fight for the Lancastrians, and in the rout following this battle, he was captured.

An account by a London citizen records that:

> 'In that battle was Owen Tudor taken, and brought unto Hereford. And he was beheaded at the market-place, and his head set upon the highest step of the market cross. And a mad woman combed his hair, and washed away the blood from his face, and she got candles and set them about him burning, more than a hundred.'

The writer explains that:

> 'This Owen Tudor . . . had wedded Queen Katharine, King Henry VI's mother. He believed and trusted all the way that he should not be beheaded, till he saw the axe and the block. And when he was in his doublet, he trusted on pardon and grace till the collar of his red velvet doublet was ripped off. Then he said: 'That head shall lie on the stock that was wont to lie on Queen Katharine's lap', and put his heart and mind wholly unto God, and full meekly took his death.'

The Welsh historian Sir Owen M. Edwards presents us with a dramatic picture of Wales during the Wars of the Roses — the little Prince of Wales, eight years old, wearing 'a pair of brigantines covered with purple velvet adorned with gold' during the Battle of St Albans. The Prince, having been knighted by his father after the battle, himself knighted eminent Lancastrians and passed judgement on the prisoners. It is difficult to believe that his mother, the redoubtable Queen Margaret, enquired of her precocious son what action to take regarding the prisoners, and that his reply, that they should all have their heads cut off, was apparently taken quite seriously.

'Throughout the dreary dynastic war,' Sir Owen continues, 'Wales was divided against itself. Welshmen fell in hundreds on the English battlefields. The archers of Gwynedd, wearing the gold and crimson, and the ostrich feathers of their prince, pushed against the blinding snowstorm which enveloped the blood-stained field of Towton. The men of Harlech held out stubbornly for Lancaster against the Yorkist Herbert when every other castle had surrendered.'

Harlech was besieged for seven years, and the castellan, Sir Dafydd ab Ieuan ap Einion, made a much-quoted comment that as a youth, he had held a castle in France for so long that every old woman in Wales had heard of it: he intended in his old age, to hold this castle in Wales, for so long that every old woman in France heard about it. In the event, the garrison managed to get their supplies by sea, and it was only when completely besieged so that they were practically at starvation point that the determined Sir Dafydd finally surrendered.

It was claimed that Henry Tudor himself was behind the walls of Harlech during the seige, but if he was, he managed to escape to Brittany, where he and his small band of followers remained in exile for fourteen years. His chief supporter and most influencial adviser was his uncle, Jasper Tudor, Earl of Pembroke (one of the sons of Owen Tudor and Katharine of France) who was to steer his nephew safely within reach of the crown of England.

Jasper seems to have been an extremely skilful PR man, and the fact that no less than thirty-five Welsh poets who were carrying on the bardic tradition during this period, all wrote about their expectations of the exiled Tudor prince, shows just how deeply Wales and the Welsh people felt involved with Henry Tudor and his claim to the throne. When at last Henry made a move, it was with the people of Wales holding their breath, as it were.

But his first attempt to come to England and claim his crown ended in failure. Henry took advantage of the rebellion by the powerful Duke of Buckingham who held lands in south-east Wales, to sail to England, but his fleet was crippled by gales. In addition, Buckingham's rebellion failed, and the Duke was executed, so that the power of King Richard III appeared to be stronger than ever.

With characteristic caution, Henry bided his time, and two years later, he was to reap the reward of his patience. In August 1485, he landed at Milford Haven with a ragged army of Normans who had been supplied by the King of France. It consisted of two or three thousand men, described by one chronicler as 'the most unruly men that could be found'. But Henry carried with him promises of support from the great English houses of Stanley and Percy and from the Welsh lord Rhys ap Thomas of Dinefwr, as well as several other lesser nobles.

Once he had landed, he progressed to Haverfordwest and then to Cardigan. Small groups who arrived to swell the ranks of his army were welcomed, but he heard to his consternation that Rhys ap Thomas and other supposed allies were actually preparing to take arms against him. It was only by the sort of cunning negotiation of which Henry was an accomplished master, that he managed to turn the lord Rhys to his side — by promising him the 'lieutenancy' in Wales when Henry became king.

As his army proceeded to Shrewsbury and through Shropshire, further assurances of assistance were forthcoming, though the Stanleys, on whom so much depended, were reluctant now that the moment was upon them, to commit themselves irrevocably to Henry's cause. It was only on the actual field of battle at Bosworth Field itself, that Sir William Stanley (treacherously, so supporters of King Richard III have claimed ever since) suddenly threw his forces on Henry's side, making a Tudor victory possible and enabling Henry to be able to win the crown.

Richard fell fighting bravely, cut off from his men in what almost amounted to single combat with his rival. Even the Court Historian who recorded the events of the battle for Henry, who was obliged to give a version that would satisfy the Tudors, could not deny that Richard III had died like a king.

'King Richard alone was killed fighting manfully in the thickest press of his enemies,' he wrote, adding: 'his courage was high and fierce and failed him not even at the death which, when his men forsook him, he preferred to take by the sword rather than, by foul flight, to prolong his life.'

Once Richard was dead, most of his forces surrendered. His body was stripped and thrown unceremoniously across the back of a horse. Later it was displayed for the common people to gawp at. But the crown which he had worn during the battle had rolled from his brow and come to rest under a thornbush. According to English tradition, it was retrieved by Lord Stanley, who placed it on the head of Henry Tudor in a triumphant 'crowning' on the battlefield itself. Welsh tradition gives this honour to Rhys ap Thomas, who is said to have been knighted as a result of his gesture of homage.

In London, the new king celebrated his victory with a *Te Deum*, and the Welsh gloried in their pride at this son of their own land who had ridden to his triumph with the red dragon of Cadwaladr fluttering for the world to see. At last they had won the greatest victory they could hope to win.

The Venetian Ambassador wrote to his government: "The Welsh may now be said to have recovered their former independence, for the most wise and fortunate Henry VII is a Welshman.' Francis Bacon wrote later of Henry: 'To the Welsh people his victory was theirs; they had thereby regained their liberty.'

Lament for the Earl of Pembroke

(William Herbert, who was killed at the Battle of Banbury in 1469. These words are also apt in the context of Henry Tudor's life.)

Yesterday he went under the black planet
through the hills yonder to fight;
trust in a feeble fate
tricked him into leaving Gwent.
Woe is me, over my poor wretch,
that he didn't stay in his own land.

Guto'r Glyn

The Act of Union

Although Henry Tudor's victory at Bosworth Field had united Wales and England, it was not until the reign of Henry VIII that this unity was made legal. Between 1536 and 1543 were passed several Acts of Parliament uniting the two countries. Wales was split into shires; the Welsh language was declared unofficial; Welsh customs and old laws were abolished.

There were certain advantages to the Welsh. The creation of the new shires meant that the old days of Marcher lords and Marcher barons had gone for ever, and government would be more stable. The Welsh were no longer regarded as troublesome second-rate peasants — by the Act of Union, they were given the status of citizens, of equal standing with English citizens. They were able to participate fully in all aspects of life in towns now, as well as in rural areas, and they had all the rights of their citizenship.

However, the fact that the official language in Wales was henceforward to be English, that Welsh would become a gabble that had no legal meaning, meant that the national identity of Wales was again threatened. Her language was part of her heritage, the language in which the bards had sung their laments and expressed their visions and dreams for as long as Wales could remember. In addition, Welshmen who could not speak English — and there were many — could not understand the new laws and regarded all officialdom as attempting to cheat them and usurp them out of their rights. Wales became heavily suspicious and resentful of impositions and restrictions passed upon it in the English language.

So once again, it was necessary to fight for freedom to speak in the Welsh tongue and have it recognised and accepted as equal with other languages. There was no immediate revolt, and no outright rebellion, since the country was now benefiting from its union with England. But over the years, the desire to be free not just to live in their own territory, stirred within the hearts of many Welshmen. They wanted to have their heritage, their individuality as Welsh people, and most of all, their literature and their language acknowledged as theirs by right and granted the dignity that was their due. So the battles of Wales still continued.

My Land

She is a rich and rare land;
O! she's a fresh and fair land;
She is a dear and rare land —
This native land of mine.

No men than hers are braver —
Her women's hearts ne'er waver;
I'd freely die to save her,
And think my lot divine.

She's not a dull or cold land;
No! she's a warm and bold land;
O! she's a true and old land —
This native land of mine.

Could beauty ever guard her,
And virtue still reward her,
No foe would cross her border —
No friend within it pine.

O, she's a fresh and fair land;
O, she's a true and rare land!
Yes, she's a rare and fair land —
This native land of mine.

Thomas Davis

Chapter Thirteen

CIVIL WAR BATTLES

In August, 1642, Charles I of England raised his standard at Nottingham, and plunged his realm into civil war. In Wales, popular feeling among the gentry, and those who were aware of the situation at Westminster, was already showing some dissatisfaction with the King's court, his powerful Catholic favourites, his methods of government. But Wales as a whole frowned on the new Puritan method of religious worship, and the Parliamentarian party was strongly Puritan, so apart from in the extreme south-west, where a pocket of Parliamentarian support was kept alive by the Devereux family, the Welsh gentry and landowners rallied loyally to the King's cause.

Their feelings were not really prompted by political bias or religious zeal. London was a long way away, and it was almost impossible to keep track of what was going on there. In Wales, opinion was that the best thing they could do for the good of their country was to keep any armies of whatever sort firmly outside the Welsh border. James Howell, a curate's son from Llangamarch, who travelled widely, wrote profusely and was later appointed Historiographer Royal to Charles II, declared that civil war would be a danger to all the peace and security the country had enjoyed for over a century. He, along with many other Welshmen, did not want to see a change in government.

The Welsh people also payed the King's levy of 'Ship Money' to build up his navy, without complaint in the early years of the war, since the money was being used to protect their coasts, particularly in the south and west. They feared that outside assistance which might be sent into Britain from the Catholic factions in Ireland or Spain, could result in the landing of foreign mercenaries on Welsh soil, and the pillaging of the whole country. There was a reluctance at first for some of the landowners to commit themselves to either the Royalist or the Parliamentarian cause, and even when they did, it was quite common during the Civil Wars for participants to change sides, sometimes more than once, as confidence in the King was undermined or the events of the war suggested wiser courses of action.

It is very obvious when maps of the campaigns and battles of the Civil Wars are consulted, that there were hardly any battles on Welsh soil which were memorable to historians or which played a significant

101

part in the eventual fate of the unfortunate King Charles and of the realm. The only battle that is usually mentioned on such maps is the Battle of Rowton Heath, which was in England — though on the border with Wales — having taking place just outside Chester on 24 September, 1645.

But Chester was a vital strategic stronghold, just as it had been in the days when Aethelfrith of Northumbria engaged the Welsh princes and their force in the Battle of Chester and slaughtered the monks who had come to pray on the battlefield.

The battles which did take place on Welsh soil, mostly concerned the investing and sieges of castles which were being held by stubborn Royalists or equally stubborn Parliamentarians, against the opposing forces. The King himself advanced to the Welsh border when civil war was declared, to recruit men for his cause, and the Welsh rallied faithfully. Welsh soldiers were in the ranks at almost all the great battles whose names ring down the centuries from the days when Roundhead fought Cavalier, and the King was heavily supported by five thousand Welsh troops at the first major engagement of the Civil War, the Battle of Edgehill in Warwickshire.

It was to commemorate those Welsh soldiers who fell at Edgehill, where they had heavy losses, that the song — or poem — 'Poor Taffy' was composed. This was published in London in 1642 as part of a pamphlet with the title: 'The Welshman's Public Recantation, or her hearty sorrow for taking up arms against her Parliament, etc.'

But this particular chapter features as its principal players, characters with names other than Charles Stuart, Oliver Cromwell or Rupert of the Rhine. One such was Sir Thomas Myddleton of Chirk Castle, MP for the then county of Denbighshire and son of a Lord Mayor of London. Sir Thomas held the rank of Sergeant-Major-General of Parliamentary Forces in North Wales, and in this capacity led troops against the Welsh Royalists in the first pitched battle of the war on Welsh soil, at Montgomery in the autumn of 1644. The previous year, he had been instrumental in seizing Wrexham, Holt, Hawarden and Flint for Parliament, and later, by one of the ironies of war, he found himself besieging Chirk Castle, his own home, which had been occupied by the Royalists during his absence.

John Watts, who was holding Chirk for the Royalist cause, sent a message dated December 25, 1644, to Prince Rupert, the King's nephew, explaining that:

'They (Sir Thomas and his troops, referred to by John Watts as

102

'the rebels') lately besieged me for three days; their engineers attempted to work into the castle with iron crows and pickers, under great planks and tables which they had erected against the castle-side for their shelter, but my stones beat them off. They acknowledged in Oswestry they had 31 slain by the castle, and 43 others hurt; their prime engineer was slain by the castle-side; they are very sad for him.'

An account of Sir Thomas' attempt to take Chirk appeared in the Royalist newspaper *Mercurius Aulicus*, which was the earliest regular English newspaper and which was produced at Oxford from 1643-1645. This explains that Sir Thomas wanted to keep the Christmas festivities that year in one of his own houses and continues:

'He came therefore before Chirk four days before Christmas, with his two brothers, Cols, Mytton and Powell. He would not abuse the castle with ordnance (because it was his own house), but fell on with fire-locks at a sink-hole where the Governor, Col. Watts, was ready to receive him; and gave a pretty number admittance (having an inner work within that hole), but when he saw his opportunity, he knocked them all down that came in, and with muskets killed of the rebels 67, wounded many more, and beat off Sir Thomas, who became so enraged that he plundered his own tenants.'

The fiery Sir Thomas had presumably not learned to control his temper any more than he had when an Irish force of ardent Royalists landed at Mostyn and forced him to retire from his conquests in North Wales. On that occasion, he not only destroyed Holt bridge, on the border, behind him as he retreated, but he also carried off the lead of the organ of Wrexham Church, in order to make bullets with it.

Local tradition in the town of Wrexham has it that it was Cromwell himself and his soldiers who stabled their horses in the Church, but it is more than likely that Cromwell never set foot in Wrexham, and Sir Thomas Myddleton was the Roundhead ogre whose name was used by exasperated mothers to threaten their naughty children.

Another Welsh hero was Colonel William Salesbury, an ardent and unswerving Royalist who fortified Denbigh Castle for the King at his own expense, and held it against all comers. He was popularly known as 'Hen Hosannau Gleision' (*Old Blue Stockings*) because he used to stump round the barricades in stockings of that out-moded shade. A man who spoke his mind, Colonel Salesbury did not even spare the King himself. When Charles Stuart came to Denbigh after his crushing defeats at Naseby and Rowton Heath, to rendezvous with his Welsh followers, and lodged at the castle, he was treated to lectures which went on for several hours from his elderly host.

Later he said wryly that: 'Never did a prince hear so much truth at once', but he bore no grudge against Colonel Salesbury, and the faithful commander of the Denbigh garrison vowed he would never yield the castle except at a direct command from Charles himself.

Later, in 1646, the castle came under siege from the troops commanded by the Major-General of the Parliamentary forces, Sir Thomas Mytton, and the town of Denbigh fell. For months, the seige dragged on, in spite of letters from Sir Thomas to Colonel Salesbury, pleading with him to surrender in order to save the inhabitants of the castle further suffering. Old Blue Stockings stood as indomitably as ever at the barricades. But he did send a message to King Charles, informing his sovereign of the current state of the siege, of the hardships his people were suffering and how his own soldiers were sick and at the limit of their resources.

The king gave the command to surrender, but on the most honourable terms. The garrison was not to be molested, robbed or insulted by the victorious Parliamentarian troops. And on 26th October, Colonel Salesbury and the gallant defenders of Denbigh marched out with their colours flying, keeping step to the beat of the drum.

The history of the Civil Wars in Wales, from the point of view of battles at least, can be summed up in stories like the one about the so-called 'Winter's leap' at Lancaut, near Chepstow, just over the border. Apparently in the early days of the Civil War, a party of Royalists under Sir John Winter were holding land here in an attempt to keep clear passage across the River Wye into Welsh territory. They were attacked at high water, and only twenty men were left alive out of a force of a hundred and eighty.

Sir John, fighting valiantly, retreated through the woods to the top of the cliff. Still pursued by the enemy, he spurred his horse over a wall, expecting that he would land in the next field — but instead of a field, there was a sheer 300-foot drop into the river. Nothing daunted, Sir John, still astride his horse, not only landed safely in the water but swam strongly to the Welsh side of the river, where he was able to make his escape.

What matters most about stories like this — stories like the Roundhead stabling of horses in Wrexham Church — is not so much whether they really happened, but what sort of impression the Civil Wars made on the ordinary people of Wales. Unlike the gentry and landowners, they did not care very much about either the King or Parliament. In fact, the situation which bothered Welsh traders most was that the King's war badly affected the cattle trade with London.

But if bards were no longer able to find a great deal of inspiration in the exploits of the various protagonists as King fought Parliament, the ordinary people repeated tales to each other of the horrors and wonders of the war, the gallant acts and the cowardly treacheries, marvelling or shuddering as each detail was repeated — and not caring at all that in the telling, the stories became so exaggerated that the traditional tales which linger today are often completely untrue. Ghostly Cavaliers still flee through the byways of Wales, retreating from equally ghostly Roundhead pursuit.

The later years of civil war turned the focus of attention on South Wales. In the north, where the Royalist cause had been defended by stalwarts such as Colonel Salesbury at Denbigh, and another excellent soldier, Sir John Owen of Clenennau, who held Conway for the King, the Royalist strongholds were systematically subdued by the Parliamentarian general Sir Thomas Mytton. His last triumphant conquest was Harlech Castle, which surrendered in March 1647. The war in North Wales was virtually over.

Sir Thomas Myddleton of Chirk Castle, that fiery besieger of his own home, was only one of the people who changed sides during the war. After twice attempting to take Chirk, which was in Royalist hands, he later found the fanaticism of the Roundheads was not to his liking, and declared for the King. As a result, he ended up besieged within the walls of Chirk himself, defending it against the artillery of his former comrades.

In the south, one of the most noted Parliamentary leaders, Rowland Laugharne of St Bride's had achieved outstanding victories in 1644 when he repulsed the Earl of Carbery's attempts to reduce Pembrokeshire, and followed this up by taking Tenby, Haverfordwest and Carmarthen from Royalist hands. As the fortunes of war ebbed and flowed, these prizes were lost to him, retrieved again and eventually sealed by his great victory — so far as local tradition in Pembrokeshire is concerned — at a stretch of moorland between Wiston and Llawhaden. Here occurred the 'Colby Moor Rout', on 1 August 1644, at which the Parliamentary forces under Laugharne held the field in a most decisive manner.

But like Sir Thomas Myddleton in the north, the Parliamentary commander Major-General Rowland Laugharne — and his fellow officers in South Wales, Major John Poyer of Pembroke and Colonel Rice Powell — found their treatment by their Parliamentary over-lords unacceptable. They too declared for the King.

Together they led a Royalist army of eight thousand men through Carmarthen into Glamorgan, capturing Swansea and Neath.

The last and most decisive battle of the Civil Wars in Wales was the Battle of St Fagans on 8 May, 1648. Laugharne and his forces were defeated overwhelmingly by the smaller but more highly trained army of the Parliamentarian Colonel Horton, who hastened to intercept them on their march to Glamorgan and did so at St Fagans.

As battles go, this was not as magnificent as the great examples of tactics displayed in other Civil War conflicts. But it had the result Colonel Horton wanted. Laugharne had placed his forces on lower ground near to a brook, and commenced by sending 500 men across it. They were beaten back by cavalry, and the whole Royalist front started to give ground. The Parliamentary cavalry attempted an encircling charge, to such good effect that within only a short time, the uncertainty in the Royalist lines had turned to panic, and the day was lost. Three thousand of Laugharne's men surrendered on the battlefield, but he and his fellow-officers managed to slip through the lines and make their way back to Pembroke.

After St Fagans, Cromwell determined to stamp out any remaining flickers of Royalist loyalty in South Wales, and he marched to take Chepstow Castle, which was being valiantly defended for the King by Sir Nicholas Kemeys. This gallant Royalist died sword in hand in the final assault by Parliamentary forces, when the defenders, already convinced the day was lost, were attempting to make their escape through the holes the Parliamentary artillery had made in the castle walls. But before the castle fell to his commander, Cromwell had already left for Pembroke, where the renegade leaders Poyer and Laugharne had established themselves.

The situation was a critical one. The Parliamentary army was engaged on the other side of the country besieging Colchester. The Scots were advancing on London. Parliament was negotiating with the king and might have come to some agreement over terms before Cromwell returned. A great deal depended on how long Pembroke could hold out for the Royalist cause. The whole future of England might have hung in the balance.

In view of the fact that he had no heavy artillery with him because the ship carrying his siege guns had been driven ashore by a storm and the guns had sunk in the sand, Cromwell decided to try and starve out the garrison. He sent to Carmarthen for shot, and ordered his big guns by sea from Gloucester.

After a few weeks, he wrote: 'They begin to be in extreme want of provision, so as in all probability they cannot live a fortnight without being starved.' There were reports that the defenders had mutinied and declared it would be better to throw their commanders over the walls. Cromwell's men pressed the castle hard but still, in spite of their starved and weakened condition, the defenders showed no signs of abandoning their commanders or giving in, and their sorties to undermine the besieging forces were carried out with desperate intensity.

Cromwell changed his mind about the defenders being starved in a fortnight, and several weeks later, at the end of June, he wrote: 'Here is a very desperate enemy, who, being put out of all hope of mercy, are resolved to endure to the uttermost extremity, being very many of them gentlemen of quality and men thoroughly resolved.'

The Parliamentary forces had destroyed the castle's water-supply, and no provisions had been brought in for a siege. By the first of July, the garrison was existing on rainwater and biscuits. Blearily, the defenders watched as Cromwell's big guns, newly arrived from Gloucester, were manoeuvred into position, and defeat stared them in the face, since their own powder was almost gone. But still they would not give in. Finally, on the 11th July when the great guns were reducing the castle walls to rubble, the exhausted garrison tiredly surrendered after withstanding a siege of seven weeks. The war in Wales was virtually over.

Heroic Civil War Castles

The Civil Wars saw the last traces of military action so far as the castles of Wales were concerned. The victorious Cromwell was thorough in 'slighting' or blowing up the sturdy walls which had held out against his troops, so that they would never again be militarily effective.

Aberystwyth Castle, for instance, which had housed the mint that produced silver coin for the King, was practically reduced to rubble. Pembroke Castle was slighted.

If not destroyed after the Civil Wars, the castles were largely allowed to fall into disrepair or were looted for other building projects, and most are now picturesque ruins. Denbigh for example still towers on its hill-top against the visitor rather than the approaching enemy, and 'Hen Hosannau Gleision', Colonel Salesbury in his blue stockings no longer walks the battlements. But at Denbigh as with most of the other castles, the scenes and the atmosphere of famous and infamous sieges are easy to reconstruct mentally.

And not all the castles were slighted or despoiled. Others have survived in all their glory, to stand as examples of what Welshmen were really fighting for during that turbulent period. Chirk Castle, the home of Sir Thomas Myddleton who both besieged and defended it during the course of the wars, remains in the hands of the Myddleton family today, for instance, and along with most of the other castles of Wales, welcomes the interested visitor.

As with Chester, where the 'King's Tower' is still pointed out on the city Walls — the tower where King Charles witnessed the defeat of his troops in the Battle of Rowton Heath before he fled into Wales — the places where the doomed monarch walked, stayed or passed are hallowed in Welsh folk-lore. And the ghost of a vengeful and bitter Cromwell stalks behind him.

Poor Taffy

Welsh losses at Edgehill were keenly felt and produced the following poem, published in 1642.

In Kinton Green
Poor Taffy was seen,
O Taffy, O Taffy;
Taffy her stood
To her knees in blood,
O do not laugh, ye;
But her was led on
With false Commission,
To her unknown;
That poor Taffy herself
Might live in health,
But her got blows for her wealth;
O Taffy, poor Taffy!

Their grievous fight,
Did make day night,
O Taffy, Taffy;
Her would be flying,
Liked not dying,
'Twas bad Epitaphe;
Her sword and spear
Did smell for fear,
And her heart were
In a cold plight;
Made Taffy outright,
His poore britches besh — te,
O Taffy, O Taffy.

108

The guns did so f—t,
Made poor Taffy start,
O Taffy, O Taffy;
Her go bare foot,
Then so go trot,
O do not laugh, ye;
For her was bang'd,
Because her had gang'd,
Under the Command
Of Array.
Who had for her pay
Many a sound great knock that day,
O Taffy, O Taffy.

Her go in frieze,
Eat bread and cheese,
O Taffy, O Taffy;
Feed with goats,
Without old groats,
O do not laugh, ye;
Had you been there,
Where her did appear,
With cold cheer
In Knapsack,
You would then alack,
For fear have turn'd back,
O Taffy, O Taffy.

Her will now invent
How to repent,
O Taffy, O Taffy;
And for want
Of words to recant,
O do not laugh, ye;
For her will be swore,
Her will do no more,
Though her be poor;
And too true
Valour her with shew,
No more in such great crew,
O Taffy, poor Taffy.

Her do conclude
In doleful mood,
O Taffy, O Taffy;
Her will weep
To goats and sheep,
O do not laugh, ye;
For her be anger,
And then hang her,
If in danger;
Her come,
Pox upon a gun,
Has spoiled her going home,
O Taffy, poor Taffy.

Chapter Fourteen

INVASION AT FISHGUARD

After the Civil Wars, there were few further actual battles on Welsh soil. Wars continued, the American colonies fought bitterly for their independence, and in Scotland the glens ran red with the blood of those who died at Glencoe and Culloden Moor.

But in February, 1797, Wales was to be the scene of the last foreign invasion of the British Isles, an incident which is generally referred to as a battle — The Battle of Fishguard — and as a result of which the Pembroke Yeomanry were allowed to wear the Fishguard battle honours. It sounds immensely impressive, but in actual fact, this whole episode was one of the greatest non-events to take place in military history. Three people were killed — largely by accident one suspects — and the most notable thing about the battle of Fishguard was the surrender of the French invaders without a battle having really been fought at all.

During the wars with France which were to continue into the next century, the French, having failed to gain command of the seas, mounted an ambitious plan to embarrass Britain by causing trouble in Ireland. It was intended that French troops would invade Bantry Bay, as well as Newcastle, where the French hoped to burn the docks; and in the west of England they would attack Bristol.

Bad weather and consequent changes of plan ensured that none of these praiseworthy objectives were realised, but on a thinly-sunlit winter day, 22nd February, 1797, the local people who might have been going about their business in the area round Fishguard, would have stared unbelievingly at the sight of three frigates — the *Resistance*, the *Constance* and the *Vengeance* — accompanied by the lugger *Vautour*, looming in a distinctly menacing fashion across the waters of the bay.

In command of the force of 1400 strong aboard these vessels (including 800 convicts who had been released from prison as 'expendable' if the invasion should fail) was the man who is one of our last protagonists in the great battles of Wales. No king, no prince, no custodian of a royal castle, he was a rather shady character called Colonel William Tate, an Irish-American who had been an artillery officer in the American War of Independence, and who at one time had been a prisoner of the British.

His troops were a motley rabble, some of them still in irons which had not been removed when they were released from prison. They were dressed in British uniform, which they wore in the optimistic hope that the peasants and under-priviledged who might view their arrival, would realise was a sign that Colonel Tate had come to lead them in a fight for the rights of the poor against the wealthy landowners. The French commanders hoped that by this means, they could spark off a nation-wide revolt of the 'peasants', and create havoc with the idea of a united Britain. This way, they reasoned, France could all the sooner succeed in winning the war.

The 'Black Legion', as the force called itself, did not create a very reassuring impression as the frigates sailed into the bay, however. In spite of the fact that the vessels were flying English flags, bystanders were able to recognise immediately that they were enemy ships, and even before they had passed St David's, the alarm had been raised. The fort at Fishguard opened fire, and the French commander, Castagnier, retreated to the safety of the open sea. Colonel Tate, on the advice of a local man who was with the force, decided to land his troops on the cliffs of Carregwastad Point, and after nightfall, by the light of a bright moon and with the assistance of a calm sea, the invaders and their supplies were ferried ashore. Carrying their long flintlock muskets, the French troops — plus two women who had accompanied the Black Legion in the capacity of laundry-maids — scrambled the two hundred feet up the cliffs, to seize Trehowel Farm, some half a mile inland, as Colonel Tate's head-quarters.

Defences were set at nearby Carwnda Rocks, and, leaving the Colonel and his men apparently on the brink of a great victory, the French frigates left early the following morning.

In the meantime, what of the valorous Welsh defenders? How did they react to the fact that they were apparently being invaded? In the first panic when the frigates were sighted and their intention realised, messages were hurriedly sent to Lord Cawdor and Colonel Milford, the commanders of the local troops of yeoman cavalry. Lord Cawdor had already retired to bed, but at the news that the French had landed, he bestirred himself and assembled such forces as he could muster, then set out for Fishguard with about four hundred men, including his own Yeoman Cavalry and members of the Cardigan Militia, Captain Ackland's Pembroke Volunteers and some sailors and customsmen from a Haverfordwest cutter. Eight small guns were transported in a cart.

The commander of the local Fishguard Fencibles, who manned the fort at Fishguard, was Lieutenant Knox. He had decided to abandon the fort and as Lord Cawdor's troops were advancing towards Fishguard, they met the Fencibles, some two hundred and fifty strong, retreating the other way in the direction of Haverfordwest.

A situation that was already beginning to turn into farce, became increasingly hilarious when, after the two commanders had consulted and tried to agree on who was in charge of combined defensive operations and what they ought to do, the only result was a sort of hysterical panic.

Lord Cawdor, who had studied tactics but who had never before been involved in a real conflict, loudly bemoaned that the Lieutenant had allowed his Fencibles to leave the fort at Fishguard undefended while they scuttled off in ignominious flight. The unfortunate Knox — smarting from this implied accusation of cowardice — responded by challenging the noble lord to a duel. It might have been pistols at dawn, except for the fact that they and their men were standing about wasting time while the French invaders were over-running the vicinity, pillaging and looting.

Lord Cawdor took overall command and advanced courageously with a total now of 575 men, against the French force of 1400, who were heavily armed. His 'army' reached Manorowen and at Carwnda Rocks was just about to walk into a French ambush. Two hundred grenadiers were in hiding, awaiting the local militia's approach, but with some sixth sense of danger — or more likely by a lucky accident of judgement — Lord Cawdor decided to withdraw to Fishguard and Goodwick and his men retreated without any confrontation or clash of arms having taken place.

This was the second night that the French invaders had spent on Welsh soil, and each 'army' sat out the long dark hours in tense uncertainty. Lord Cawdor was probably racking his brains over the theories of military strategy he had studied, weighing up the various courses of action he could take, and it is doubtful whether he got much sleep. On the other hand, Colonel Tate had more mundane and immediate problems on his mind with regard to the behaviour of the unruly rabble under his command.

The invading force had been provided with the most up to date muskets and plenty of ammunition, but they had no horses to transport them far from their head-quarters and they had only been issued with the barest minimum of provisions. General Hoche, the French commander who had master-minded the invasion, had made it clear that resourceful Frenchmen ought to have no trouble in acquiring both transport and food and drink once they had landed on enemy soil.

Somehow, though, Colonel Tate's gallant band had not proved to be as resourceful as the General had optimistically anticipated. They had indeed set out in foraging parties from their head-quarters at Trehowel Farm, and ransacked the local farms and inns for provisions. But already there were mutterings of discontent. Colonel Tate, obviously not one those leaders of men who can rise to great heights in times of emergency, was having second thoughts about the viability of the whole enterprise and even seems to have suffered a change of heart and regretted he had agreed to come on the expedition at all.

This attitude was reflected in the behaviour of his men. They felt they had been deserted by the frigates, which ought by rights to have stayed in the vicinity to give them some sort of moral support, if nothing else, and what was worst of all, they were ravenous because of the short rations, and desperate for food. They would have been an unruly force at best, but with good reason for grievance, since they considered they had been badly treated, they turned into an undisciplined mob.

The day after they had landed, small parties of soldiers roamed the area without any attempt at concealment and with no apparent purpose except to loot all the farms they happened across. Their main objective was food and drink. They killed livestock and carried off the carcases. Most of the local people wisely kept their distance, but there were several incidents where the invaders and the angry farmers came to blows.

The French found no transport, but they did get food, and what was even more significant, there was no shortage of liquid refreshment. While the people of Fishguard would have been horrified if they had been accused of being wreckers, they nevertheless made sure that if any wrecks did occur, the fruits of such acts of God were not allowed to go to waste, and only a few weeks previous to the invasion, a Portuguese coaster carrying large quantities of Portuguese wine had come to grief on the rocks, with the result that all the farms in the vicinity were plentifully supplied with port.

The men of the Black Legion, already feeling disgruntled because the frigates had abandoned them to their fate, and with their expectations of victory at a low ebb, seized enthusiastically on the bottles of wine and commenced some serious drinking in an effort to bolster their courage. The result was that within a few hours, the whole 1400 officers and men (though apparently not Colonel Tate) were roaring drunk. It is recorded that at Brestgarn Farm, one grenadier opened fire in a spirit of bravado and claimed he had killed a member of Lord Cawdor's troops. In fact, his victim was the farmer's grandfather clock, which must have looked particularly menacing to the drunken Frenchman.

It was obvious to Colonel Tate as the night of Thursday, 23rd February, drew on, that his force was out of his control and that even if he had managed to get them to fight, they would have been quite incapable of doing anything in their present condition. The invasion was lost; the French cause was hopeless. In addition, in spite of the livestock and poultry they had slaughtered, the French were still ravenously hungry, and some of them wanted to surrender so that they could get food.

Accounts of how the surrender actually came about, vary. Some authorities claim that Colonel Tate signed a surrender note on the Thursday evening and that when it was sent to Lord Cawdor at Fishguard, he agreed to accept the surrender the next day. In other accounts, more emphasis is laid on Lord Cawdor's brilliant plant (thought out as a result of his study of tactics, no doubt) whereby he attempted to bluff the French that their numbers were greatly inferior to his own. In some cases, no mention is made of the message of surrender, but a vivid picture is painted of Lord Cawdor's advance on Goodwick Sands on the Friday morning, his troops accompanied by large numbers of Welsh women in their red cloaks and tall hats who wanted to cheer their men to victory.

It is generally agreed that the French mistook the women in their distinctive red cloaks, for extra soldiers, and there are even tales that Lord Cawdor, that military genius, organised a march-past of the women round and round a rock so that it looked as though a huge force was coming to his assistance. But almost certainly none of these theatrical tactics were necessary, as Colonel Tate could have had no hope after the fiasco of the previous day, of achieving anything except honourable terms for the surrender.

The surrender was signed that morning at the Royal Oak inn in Fishguard and the great invasion was over. But not only Lord Cawdor was the hero of the hour. More picturesque is the lady who was afterwards hailed as 'the General of the Red Army', a fearsome woman called Jemima Nicholas who had been one of Lord Cawdor's 'extras' in red cloaks and tall hats. No delicate heroine, Jemima was actually a cobbler and was tall and stout. She — as well as some of the other women — had come to the assistance of the militia armed with a pitchfork, which she proceeded to put to good use. Single-handed, she captured twelve Frenchmen in a field near to Llanwnda and marched them at pitchfork-point to the custody of the militia in Fishguard. And then she sallied forth to round up a few more. This indomitable lady lived to the ripe old age of eighty-two, and when she died in 1832, the tombstone erected in her name outside the Church of St Mary in Fishguard (still to be seen) bore the legend:

In memory of
JEMIMA NICHOLAS
of this town
THE WELSH HEROINE
who boldly marched to meet
the French Invaders
who landed on our shores in
February 1797

The abject French, having laid down their arms, were removed to Haverfordwest and imprisoned temporarily in the castle and in various churches, but though the invasion had fizzled ignominiously to nothing, the potential danger to the safety and peace of Britain if it had succeeded was not lost on the government in Westminster. Jemima Nicholas and her band of Amazonian warriors with pitchforks had apparently had to be forcibly restrained from lynching the whole 1400 of the Black Legion, and in London, news of the invasion and all that it portended sent the money market into chaos. The government suspended payments of gold and silver, and issued paper notes, which were pronounced legal tender. This practice was of course to be continued by future governments to the detriment of the economy — so in spite of the gallantry of Lord Cawdor and his self-appointed right-hand woman Jemima Nicholas, perhaps the last invasion of Britain did not altogether result in a Welsh victory.

The Ballad of the French Invasion
(a Welsh ballad to be sung on the air 'Belisle March')

The ships sailed and landed near Fishguard
To plunder and steal,
The most vicious men were the most forward
And lashing their steel.

They slaughtered calves and raided the barns,
Stole pigs and sheep,
They went to the cellars and drank the beer,
Fell in drunken sleep.

But with the morning dawn, the men of Pembroke
Rose against the foe,
With scythes and sickles, their sticks and pitchforks
To battle they did go.

And facing their fierce faces with the sun
The Frenchmen found
How in this ancient land, which is their right,
The Welsh will hold their ground.

Chapter Fifteen

THE LAST BATTLES

Swords, battle-flags and the trappings of war as Welshman faced a mortal enemy on the very soil of Wales, pass now into the realms of history and legend. In the century following the Battle of Fishguard, the struggles which took place were of a different nature, and were fought against social injustice and tyranny, rather than against a physical foe. Wales had never been conquered, and even though she accepted the overlordship of the English crown, she would not tolerate the exploitation or humiliation of her people.

The idea of the French invasion had been to encourage the 'peasants' and working classes to rise against the landowners, who were largely English or Anglicized Welsh and who understood little (and did not want to understand) of the real *Cymry*. It might have been expected that the Welsh, inspired by the events of the Revolution in France, the poor and the oppressed toppling the monarchy to seize control of their country for themselves, would have reacted in sympathy. They too were suffering extreme hardship and discontent in the nineteenth century. Life was not easy and there was a mounting pressure and agitation towards political reform which would give the workers and the rising lower-middle classes some sense of self-respect and dignity as well as ensuring they were fairly treated by their employers and fairly paid.

This was the century of trade wars, the birth of the trade unions, Chartism. When the social unrest could not be contained but bubbled up in seething fury, there were riots in Wales. There was no Revolution as such — the French invasion and the very real dangers this might have heralded had come too close to home — but infuriated Welshmen, driven to desperation by the terrible conditions under which they were forced to work, the poverty and suffering of their families, the social injustices that cried aloud for reform, took up arms in whatever manner they could to fight for their rights, their ideals, their culture, their traditions and their fair country.

The most picturesque protagonists in the 'battles' — or series of battles — which were fought during this period were known as 'Rebecca' and her 'daughters'. In the years between 1839 and 1843, the discontents of the people found an outlet as the mysterious 'Rebecca', on a white horse, rode through the night at the head of her 'daughters', the axes and flaring torches they carried signifying the destruction they inflicted wherever they felt injustice was being done.

But before the 'Rebecca Riots' broke out, there had been other notable insurrections by the Welsh to protest against the hardship and poverty in which the working classes and peasantry had to live, and their exploitation by landowners and employers. The worst discontent was felt in South Wales, particularly in the booming industrial towns and cities, though even on the land the increase in enclosures by wealthy landowners meant that small farmers and agricultural workers were having their livelihood seized from them. Bad harvests, falling prices and the new Poor Law legislation all added to the increasingly gloomy picture, and the farmers and workers turned into desperate men as they watched their families weaken and their children die from malnutrition and disease, and remained helpless.

The situation in a place like Merthyr Tudful, dominated as it was by the great iron works which had changed the countryside around from a picturesque valley to a teeming and frantic town where nothing seemed to matter to the owners except higher and higher production, at the cost of the workers if necessary, held little that was uplifting or hopeful for the ironworkers and their families. Even if working conditions had been improved, there were still innumerable social injustices which kept them subservient and repressed. The Welsh sought solace in their chapels and in the same outlet that had over the centuries kept the legends and traditions of their land alive as the bards wandered from hall to hall — music.

But it was not enough to combat sickness and injustice. In May, 1831, dissatisfaction over wage cuts and an increasing urge for reform drove the workers of Merthyr to march behind a huge white banner to a mass meeting on the hills above Dowlais. From this point onwards, the celebrated Merthyr Rising gathered momentum, and the authorities were powerless to stop it,

Although many voices were raised in the storm of protest, the Rising had no clear leader at the start, but one soon emerged after the initial clashes between the rioters and the authorities. His name was Lewis Lewis of Penderyn, and the Welsh called him Lewsyn yr Heliwr — *Lewis the Huntsman*. It appears that he was as romantic a figure as the English Robin Hood, and that as he led his bands of faithful followers against the King's men — notably the officers of the Court of Requests and the bailiffs who all too often descended on the households of those who could not pay their debts, to ransack and remove the most valuable items — he would ensure that even these enemies of his people were honourably treated.

In the early hours of the riot, while the violence was still simmering but had not yet erupted, it was a trunk belonging to Lewsyn yr Heliwr, which had been taken from his house as surety for a debt of £18.19.0d, that triggered off the insurrection. A crowd descended on the house of the shopkeeper who had taken the trunk, and dragged it away. It was placed in the open road, and Lewis himself climbed on to it and delivered a ringing and inflamatory speech in Welsh. The crowd, eager for further action, surged off and shortly afterwards, the house belonging to the president of the Court of Requests was attacked with fireballs and the windows broken.

By now, the crowds were marching with banners, some natural leaders having emerged from their ranks. Lewsyn yr Heliwr, in the front rank, was accompanied by his rescued trunk, carried as a sort of talisman by two sturdy followers. Other commanders of the Welsh 'force' were David Jones, a miner whose mates called him Dai Solomon, and another David whose surname was Thomas but who is remembered in the history of the rising as Dai Llaw-Haearn — *Dai Iron-Hand*.

Along with the banners, the crowd carried a Red Flag impaled with a loaf of bread, as well as a horn, while Dai Iron-Hand brandished his pick-axe handle with authority as he issued orders. The 'army' surged through Merthyr and systematically restored property which had been removed by the Court of Requests, to its rightful owners. A few of the more shady sort of characters attempted to do a little pilfering on their own behalf, but in general, the riot was kept within the bounds of what was felt to be decent and honest 'reform', though some shops were almost ruined by this wholescale appropriation and removal of goods and property.

By the time the authorities had mustered 'specials' and alerted the 93rd Foot at Brecon — with a plea to the commander to come immediately if it was necessary — the rising was growing in momentum, and huge armies intent on redressing the wrongs of injustice and the Court of Requests were roaming the roads under their banners. The trouble was that the authorities did not know what they wanted. They were obviously rebelling, but against what? They had made no demands, posed no ultimatums. The magistrates sent a report to the Home Office that they could discover no distinct grounds for complaint.

119

But the shopkeepers, businesses in ruins, were not prepared to wait around to find what these complaints were. They gathered in a body and demanded that the troops should be sent for immediately. And when iron-master William Crawshay arrived at the Castle Inn, where tales were coming in by the minute of fresh violence, smashing of the house of the president of the Court of Requests and burning of his furniture in the street, he wasted no time. Urgent messages were sent to Brecon to summon the 93rd Foot, the Argyll and Sutherland Highlanders; to Llantrisant for the Glamorgan Yeomanry. Specials were mustered, mostly from the ranks of the dispossessed shop-keepers.

As the morning of Friday, 3rd June, 1831 broke, about eighty Highlanders of the 93rd Foot were making a forced march over the Brecon Beacons to come to the assistance of the authorities in Merthyr. They arrived at around ten o'clock and were met by ironmaster William Crawshay and the magistrates, who led them past the massed crowd clustered beneath its banner of 'Reform'.

At the Castle Inn, the ranks of authority, magistrates, ironmasters, the High Sheriff of Glamorgan, with the Highlanders to support them, faced the huge crowds of angry workers and their women and children, which were swelling by the minute. The leaders of the uprising were there, Lewsyn yr Heliwr, Dai Solomon, and others who had come to prominence as the insurrection had gathered force.

Attempts were made to quieten the crowd, to choose delegates for talks with the authorities. But no satisfactory solution to the grievances of the workers could be achieved, though various speakers including the ironmaster Josiah John Guest tried to pour oil on the troubled waters. The crowd became more agitated, and at last began to attack the ranks of Highlanders and break them up. The resulting conflict, as the angry and frustrated mob attempted to surge into the Castle Inn, only to be driven back again and again by the Highlanders, let the pent-up fury of the rioters loose.

In the rooms above, some of the soldiers watched helplessly, their muskets at the ready, but no order was given for them to fire. Bayonets, clubs and cudgels were doing damage among the crowds below and when at last an officer shouted to the men in the inn to fire, and they were able to shoot into the turmoil, the horrifying scene which was revealed as the smoke cleared included bodies bleeding at the feet of the rioters.

Desperate moments indeed. And the clash of arms was not over.

Having come this far, the rioters were not prepared to give up now. They did not know exactly what it was that they wanted — except that the name of 'Reform' covered all the wrongs, the deprivations, the injustices, the grievances, that they had suffered for a long time — but they would not back down now that they were actually face to face with the musket barrels of hated authority, and they were taking action far beyond the limits of their power. Again and again the soldiers dispersed charging men, and again and again the mob reformed and threw itself desperately at the guns.

Attacks were made at the back of the Inn as well as the front, and the mob was so incensed that when the rioters ran out of shot for the muskets they had captured, they continued to fire marbles. At last, reluctantly, the shooting became spasmodic, and a dreadful hush fell over this battleground that had been the iron-working town of Merthyr.

The result of the riot was that sixteen of the soldiers were wounded, some severely. Casualties among the people of Merthyr were difficult to determine, as many of the wounded crept or crawled away to die secretly, in fear of reprisals against their families. The total of civilian dead was given 'authentically' as sixteen, though it was almost certainly more, and might have been much higher, since there were thought to be over seventy wounded. As the days passed, as those mortally wounded breathed their last and were silently and quickly buried in ditches, in fields, anywhere out of sight of the authorities, the rioters, more tight-lipped and determined than ever, set up armed camps, military-style, on the Brecon and Swansea road. At the thought that they might be about to rouse the whole coalfield to exact vengeance for the events at Castle Inn, and in fear of an insurrection which might number anything up to a hundred thousand workers, the authorities sent for assistance to London, where the King himself was informed of the situation. As a result, the reinforcements ordered to Merthyr included the 3rd Dragoons and 150 men of the 98th Foot, the latter embarking from Plymouth on the steam packet *Albion*, their destination Cardiff.

Beneath a blood-stained banner, the rioters now set out, grimly determined on vengeance. They seized guns, powder and shot, and armed themselves. Their ranks were swelled by the more cautious workers who had so far kept out of the riot. They began to organise themselves like an army, with commanders, battle-flags, separate detachments. They set up road-blocks and closed the roads. On the

Saturday, they rallied thousands more to their cause, and spread out into the surrounding countryside.

For a few days, it must have seemed as though the men of Merthyr, by sheer determination and in the face of all odds, might have changed the course of history. But on the Monday following the riot outside the Castle Inn, the insurrection began to fail as more and more men drifted away or split the ranks of the rioters. The military were now everywhere, and during Monday evening and the following night, fourteen 'wanted' men, leaders of the rising, were rounded up. On Tuesday Lewsyn yr Heliwr was dramatically arrested after a chase to pin him down in the woods near his home. In the dark hours of Wednesday morning, he was escorted into Merthyr by a force of yeomanry and dragoons. Along with twenty-six other prisoners, he ended up in Cardiff jail and the last flicker of rebellion against authority took place when Dai Solomon, one of the leaders of the rising, led the prisoners in a protest riot.

The rising left Merthyr and the whole area in the same miserable condition it had been in previously, but made worse because of tensions and ill feeling in the town, not to mention the deaths that had occurred and the damage that had been done. Enormous bills had been run up by the military which required settlement, along with the compensation that had yet to be agreed for lost homes and damage to property.

At the Glamorgan Summer Assizes in Cardiff the rioters were tried and Lewsyn yr Heliwr was condemned to death, but this sentence was later commuted to transportation. Other men who had taken part in the rising were also sentenced to transportation, but the real martyr of the insurrection — in the minds of the Welsh at least — was a twenty-three-year-old miner called Richard Lewis, better known in Welsh folk-history as Dic Penderyn.

Dic and Lewsyn were tried jointly on the charge of stabbing and wounding a private soldier. Lewsyn's sentence was commuted to transportation as we have heard, but the unfortunate Dic was publicly hanged in Cardiff on 13th August. He was attended on the scaffold by no less than four ministers, and huge crowds followed his corpse to Aberafon where he was buried outside the Church of St Mary's. Legends grew around his name from that moment on. He had suffered death for his part in the risings — he had given his life in the cause of reform, trade unionism and the rights of working men. It was recollected that in his life, he had beaten up a bullying constable who was known to indulge in blackmail; he was a defender of the people.

But the real reason why the name of Dic Penderyn will never be forgotten is that, almost as soon as the verdict had been passed and he had been condemned to die, it began to be made public by everyone including the ironmaster John Josiah Guest, that the crime for which he had been condemned had almost certainly been committed by someone else, and that he had been guiltless of stabbing the soldier. He continued to protest his innocence even on the scaffold, but in spite of petitions and the evidence of new witnesses, which were hurriedly prepared to try and save him, in spite of his execution (originally fixed for 30th July) being postponed until 13th August, in spite of the tide of popular feeling which focussed on his life as somehow symbolic of all that the workers were fighting for, in spite of all these, he died at the rope's end. His last word, from the scaffold, was a shout of 'Injustice', and it is said that a white bird, symbolic presumably of his innocence, alighted on his coffin.

At the end of the 1830s, existing causes for discontent in Wales were pushed to rebellion point once more when new toll-gates were erected and tolls demanded for passing along the roads controlled by the turnpike trusts. The first gate to be attacked and destroyed was at Efail-wen, and after it was re-erected, the mob struck again and attacked both the gate and the toll-house. This was to mark the beginning of the reign of terror of 'Rebecca' and her daughters, otherwise known as the Rebecca Riots.

It was mainly the country people, farmers and farm labourers, who suffered from the tolls — and who were already suffering extreme hardship from bad harvests. They attacked the hated gates in gangs, disguised in women's clothes and with blackened faces. The leader of the early risings was Thomas Rees, a pugilist known as Twm Carnabwth, after the name of his small farm. He, so the story goes, could not find women's clothes to fit him so he borrowed some from his neighbour, who happened to be called Big Rebecca. And at the gate, as the mob attacked with their flaring torches, witnesses heard this gigantic leader in a woman's dress called 'Becca' by 'her daughters'.

The theatrical drama, as well as the genuine feeling that they were trying to right a wrong, spread over the whole of south-west Wales. Bands of 'daughters', each led by a different 'Rebecca', generally riding a white horse, enacted solemn and ritualistic ceremonies before the gates they were about to destroy, prior to wrecking them. When the gates were re-erected, Rebecca and her followers would return again and again to break them down once more.

As their fervour spread, the gangs began to attempt to put right other wrongs, as well as ridding their highways of the notorious toll-gates and the tolls that crippled them, and which they could not pay. They began to take action over the new workhouses, which were much resented; they forcibly reconciled couples who were separated, 'persuaded' fathers to take responsibility for their illegitimate off-spring, and sternly warned children who were wayward of the consequences of disobeying their parents.

By 1843, Rebecca and her daughters no longer felt they needed to keep their activities in darkness, nor ride abroad by night. A crowd marched into Carmarthen to attack the Workhouse, their ranks swelled by the poor people of the town. A report in the newspaper *Welshman* of a proclamation purported to have been made by Rebecca herself claimed that the counties of Carmarthen, Cardigan and Pembroke were with her 'to a man'.

'Oh yes,' Rebecca declared, 'they are all my children' and went on to list the oppressed, the workers in their sweat, the poor in their hunger. All these, she said 'are members of my family, these are the oppressed sons and daughters of Rebecca.'

In 1844, Rebecca achieved her victory. Legislation was passed to alleviate the worst of the grievances of the Welsh against the toll-gates. But many other wrongs remained, many other causes for which in former days the Princes would have musterered their armies, simmered below the surface of Welsh consciousness, only subsiding slowly. No longer did the clash of arms break the peace of the valleys. Welsh defenders took to the polling booths, to the orator's platform and to the journalist's pen.

But the tradition of commemorating the Welsh love of their land lingers on even today in the songs and laments of Welshmen who feel 'hiraeth' or homesickness tugging at them even across the sea. After the Rebecca Riots, Dai'r Cantwr (*Dai the Singer*), one of the leaders who was condemned to transportation to Tasmania (Van Diemen's Land) wrote these haunting lines:

Dai Cantwr's Song of Longing
(Sung in Welsh in Carmarthen Jail)

Far from my country, I will be sent
Away, from my father's lands,
A tear or two will drown my eyes
As irons clasp my hands.

For twenty years or more I'll not
Her shores or rivers see,
Young I will go, but with a heavy heart,
Old coming home I'll be.

Farewell to the garden of the world,
And the fair young maids so fine
Farewell Glamorgan and Bridge-end
I'm crossing over the brine.

And if any one will hold your arm
And ask who the poet be
Who cried his sorrow in this song,
Dai Cantwr, boys, that's me.

Still in the mountains, the valleys, the hearts of her people, the armies of Wales will muster whenever this lovely land is threatened, though the sword appears to be stilled.

BIBLIOGRAPHY OF SELECT WORKS CONSULTED

Carr, A.D., *Llywelyn ap Gruffydd* (University of Wales Press, 1982).

Chadwick, Nora K., *Celtic Britain*, (Thames & Hudson, 1963).

Chadwick, Nora K., 'The Battle of Chester: A Study of Sources'. In *Celt and Saxon — Studies in the Early British Border* (Cambridge University Press, 1963).

Dodd, A.H., *A Short History of Wales: Welsh Life and Customs from prehistoric times to the present day* (Batsford, 1977).

Edwards, Owen M., Wales (T. Fisher Unwin Ltd., 1925).

Featherstone, Donald, *The Bowmen of England* (New English Library, 1973).

Gillingham, John, *The Wars of the Roses* (Weidenfeld and Nicolson, 1981).

Inglis-Jones, Elisabeth, *The Story of Wales* (Faber 1955).

John, Brian, *Pembrokeshire* (Pan Books Ltd., 1978).

Jones, Bedwyr Lewis, *Arthur y Cymru — The Welsh Arthur* (University of Wales Press 1973).

Kinross, John, *The Battlefields of Britain* (David & Charles, 1979).

Kinross, John, *Walking and Exploring the Battlefields of Britain* (David & Charles, 1988).

Nicholle, David, *Arthur and the Anglo-Saxon Wars: Anglo-Celtic Warfare AD 410-1066* (Osprey Publishing, 1984).

Owen, Dilys, *Holywell: A Traveller's Companion* (Wyn Williams, 1968).

Rhys, J., *Celtic Britain* (SPCK Brighton, 1884).

Rothero, Christopher, *The Scottish and Welsh Wars 1250-1400* (Osprey Publishing, 1984).

Skidmore, Ian, *Owain Glyndŵr, Prince of Wales* (Christopher Davies, 1978).

Smurthwaite, David, *The Ordnance Survey Complete Guide to the Battlefields of Britain* (Webb & Bower Publishers Ltd., 1984).

The Sphere Illustrated History of Britain C55BC-1485 (Sphere Reference, 1985).

Tacitus, *The Annals*.

Tacitus, *The Agricola*.

Warner, Philip, *Famous Welsh Battles* (Fontana/Collins 1977).

Williams, David, *A History of Modern Wales* (John Murray, 1950).

Williams, Gwyn, *The Land Remembers: A View of Wales* (Faber and Faber, 1977).

Williams, Gwyn A., *The Merthyr Rising* (Croom Helm Ltd., 1978).

ACKNOWLEDGEMENTS

'The Eagles Depart' — translation by D.M. Lloyd.
'The Hall in Darkness' — translation by Ernest Rhys.
'Sleep, Gwenllian' — translation by A.P. Graves.
'The Battle of Tal-y-Moelfre' — translation by Joseph P. Clancy.
'In Praise of Llywelyn ab Iorwerth' — translation by Joseph P. Clancy.
'Lament for Llywelyn ap Gruffudd' — translation by Joseph P. Clancy.
'The Exile of Cambria' — translation by A.P. Graves.
'Men of Harlech' — translation by A.P. Graves.